Case Studies in Communication

before the last date shown below.

2⁹

Case Studies in Communication

-4 JUN 1999

GRAHAM COLLINS

PITMAN PUBLISHING
128 Long Acre, London WC2E 9AN

© Graham Collins 1987

First published in Great Britain 1987

British Library Cataloguing in Publication Data

Collins, Graham
    Case studies in communication.
    1. Communication in management——Case
    studies
    I. Title
    651.7'0722   HF5718

    ISBN 0 273 02545 7

Photoset in 10pt Palatino by 𝔽\ Tek Art Limited, Croydon.

Printed and bound in Great Britain at the Bath Press, Avon.

Contents

Acknowledgements

My sincere thanks are due to the following organisations and individuals for the assistance they have given me in the writing of this book:

The Woolwich Equitable Building Society, the French Travel Service, the Institute of Marketing, Derek Maynard and Associates Ltd, Midland Bank plc, the London Chamber of Commerce and Industry, Frantour, the Industrial Society, Army and Navy Stores Ltd, the Institute of Administrative Management, the Royal Society of Arts, the *South East London Mercury*, the London Borough of Lewisham, *The Grocer*, the Economist Intelligence Unit. I am indebited to Joy Rebello for typing the manuscript.

Thanks of an entirely different sort are sincerely expressed to Harry Bridges, Harley Davies, Charlotte Feinmann and Marina Collins.

L

General Introduction

A case study is a record of an episode or situation that is used as a basis for learning by means of study, discussion and decision. The episode or situation may be entirely real or entirely imaginary. In this book the case studies belong between these two poles: each one is an extension or clarification of a real episode, adapted in order to improve learning potential.

Case study learning is very widely used in commercial and industrial training today, and first gained widespread attention when used at the Harvard Business School in the United States. All the cases in this book have a realistic basis and have been designed in consultation with a wide range of organisations and professional bodies, in both the public and the private sector. The aim of the book is to present a series of cases that may either be studied independently, or as an integrated course. In either case the aim is to enable students to study Communication in an applied context, focusing on problems and breakdowns in the communication process that occur in each of the varied settings. To support the consideration of each case, there are a number of student exercises which will develop practical communication skills. These exercises may be taken together, or used selectively. Each chapter is built around one case, and organised in four related stages as follows:

1 *Introduction* – the facts and background of each case.

2 *Analysis* – the stage of the exercise where the users, individually or collectively, should consider the issues of the case study. This stage involves such considerations as the following:

- Ranking the issues in order of importance or seriousness.
- Identifying the relationship between the different issues of each case.
- Distinguishing primary from secondary causes.

3 *Planning and solving* – having analysed the problem, the student's thinking must now generate one or a number of possible solutions, and identify the 'plus' and 'minus' factors for each one. Standard criteria for provoking this stage of thinking could be:

- What is to be accomplished?

- What is to be corrected?
- What is to be improved?
- What is to be eliminated?

Each study provides criteria for this stage of the exercise. Some chapters involve role play and the solution of the same case from differing angles.

4 Each case finishes with an 'Exercises' section, in which a number of performance assignments are set that may be used selectively or comprehensively. Each assignment exercises a particular communication skill, usually either spoken or written, based on the case itself.

Answers are not given to the problems raised by the cases, except in the first chapter, as there is rarely one definitive 'answer'. Study and discussion will produce a range of possible treatments of problems, and hopefully consensus will select the most appropriate 'answer'.

The assignments have been designed and varied throughout the book in order to exercise and develop a range of communication skills appropriate to the requirements of courses such as the BTEC National module, People and Organisations, the Royal Society of Arts Examinations in Communication in Business at Stage One and at Stage Two, the AEB Ordinary/Alternative Level examination in English for Professional and Business Use and other secretarial and professional examinations. Finally, there is a glossary of terms used in the book, and sources for obtaining further case studies are given.

I hope that the book will prove useful either as a central course manual, or as a source for reference or occasional use.

Table of communication skills

Case	Visual and graphical	Written	Listening and speaking	Researching and reading
1 Householder Building Society	✓	✓		
2 The French Connection		✓	✓	✓
3 Stainton and Wrigland		✓	✓	✓
4 Automation at Midwest	✓	✓	✓	
5 Crisis at Comlon	✓	✓	✓	
6 Recruitment at Carefree	✓	✓	✓	✓
7 Tartan Fashions	✓	✓	✓	✓
8 Minitron	✓	✓		
9 Gondola Chain		✓	✓	
10 Beaumanor Golf Club (1)	✓	✓		
11 Beaumanor Golf Club (2)		✓	✓	
12 Southden Housing Department	✓	✓		
13 Asmart: The Spring Offensive	✓	✓		✓

1 · The Householder Building Society

This case study is designed to exercise the following skills:

1 Appreciation of the stages in the communication process and the many chances of breakdown.
2 Ability to identify points of communication breakdown.
3 Ability to detect and represent the communication structure of an organisation.
4 Ability to detect, distinguish and rank the causes of a problem.
5 Ability to distinguish between central, regional and local operations of an organisation.
6 Ability to produce an organisation chart.
7 Ability to produce an appropriately presented briefing paper (without recommendations).
8 Ability to produce a diagnostic report (with recommendations).
9 Ability to produce a discussion document appropriate in layout and content for senior management.
10 Ability to control content and tone in specialised types of letter (letter of apology, letter of conciliation).

Notes for teachers

This case study is based on a communication breakdown at several levels: between the Board of Directors and senior/middle management (in this case, the Public Relations Department of the society), between branch management and branch staff and between branch management and area management.

The skills of the student are tested in the areas of analysis and planning and solving, and by exercises.

Analysis

Identifying the breakdowns of communication at the levels of occurrence and differentiating the problems into local (branch staff and branch management), regional (branch management and area management) and central (Board of Directors and senior management). In order to perform this analysis, the student will need some understanding of the complex and multiple lines of communication that operate in a large, nationally active organisation, and such awareness should develop as the case study is worked. From the evidence in the preliminary description of the case study, it will be possible to make deductions about the cause or causes into primary/ secondary, possible/probable order, and to distinguish between causes provoked by the policy of the company, by its existing internal structure and by its operations at branch and Head Office level.

Planning and solving

By completing an analysis the student has 'processed' the problem to the point where he/she has a list of causes, which are categorised in at least two ways:

(a) They are defined as having originated *centrally*, *regionally* or *locally*.

(b) They are ranked in order of having been caused by *policy*, *structure/organisation*, or by particular *operational* failings in a particular 'area' of the firm's activities.

From this point, the student will go on to generate one or more possible treatments for each problem, and will outline likely benefits, drawbacks and repercussions of each course. This is the most testing area of this case study in terms of individual application by the student, and it will feature less guidance from the text than either of the other sections. However, the student's input will be linked with the preliminary 'compulsory' consideration of what is to be corrected/ accomplished/eliminated/improved. All these considerations will be constrained by the factors expressed in the case study itself, and the student will also have to rank these objectives in order of importance.

Exercises

1 Producing an organisation chart of the company that highlights areas of operational/structural weakness.
2 Preparing and presenting a diagnostic report on the problems experienced in the campaign at branch level (local operational failures) that could be corrected locally, with approval by management at regional level.
3 Producing an information report researching the legal implications of campaigns involving young children (for the Board of Directors).
4 Producing a discussion document for the Board of Directors on

(a) Advantages/disadvantages of adhering to present policy/campaign.
(b) Benefits/drawbacks of policy changes.
(c) Range of policy changes immediately available.
(d) Impact of each policy change on existing practices.

5   Writing a letter of conciliation to parents of 'victim' of campaign (communication task for branch manager).

Summary

The chapter attempts to do the following:

1   Involve the student in serious thought and work on the variety of communication problems that may beset a large organisation at a number of *different*, but *related* areas, as a result of one issue or campaign. (Analysis.)
2   Involve a range of problem-solving activities, which include choices of priorities and judgements, as to the order of importance of each one solution, with final choice of 'best' solution. (Planning and solving.)
3   Having selected a solution, the student should then produce

  (a) An organisation chart.
  (b) A diagnostic report.
  (c) A discussion document.
  (d) A letter of apology/conciliation/adjustment.

Introduction

The Householder Building Society, first established in Winchester, Hampshire, in 1967, now has seven branches, which are organised in three regions, corresponding to the boundaries of the English counties in which they are situated.

The Hampshire region has three branches: at Winchester (Head Office, PO Box 500, Winchester, Hants); Southampton (14 Water Prospect, Southampton); and Portsmouth (140 Wellington Road, Portsmouth). The Hampshire region is under the control of Mr Adrian Reid, Regional Manager. The job of a regional manager is to co-ordinate the activities of all branches in his region, to make monthly reports to the Director of Marketing and Development at Head Office, and to integrate the operation of branches by making suitable and appropriate movements of staff from one branch to another, in order to maintain career development for the Society's employees. The Regional Manager also assesses the performance of each of the branches under his control and advises the branch manager in meetings held at least monthly on the premises of each branch. He is also responsible for maintaining communication with branch managers, by explaining the decisions, policy and plans of the Board of Directors to them at monthly meetings. The Dorset region is controlled by Alison Wilks and covers the company's two branches in

Dorset, in Lyme Regis and Weymouth. The third region is the Wiltshire region, with one branch in Salisbury and one in Trowbridge. Mark Beale is the Regional Manager.

Because the society is relatively small and has few branches, the regional managers are all based at Head Office in Winchester. This enables them to spend some of their time working on administrative tasks for the Society as a whole, and the remainder of their time on their own region. This arrangement was made as the regions are too small, with too few branches, to occupy fully a senior member of staff. However, the directors firmly support the idea of regionalisation as it promotes healthy competition between regions.

The Society hopes, over a three-year period, to expand a total of 10–12 offices, by opening at least one new office in each region, and possibly two offices in those regions that demonstrate they possess the quality of management and the market potential for such expansion. This project is organised by Roland Hayday, the Director of Marketing and Development at Head Office.

The policy of the Society is to make an impact in the lending market by remaining a small operation and developing a reputation for quality of service. This is achieved by processing loan applications very quickly, and by carefully maintaining excellent customer relations. Courtesy, thoroughness and, above all, a friendly and receptive atmosphere within each branch of the Society are the foundations of this strategy.

Each branch of the Society is staffed in exactly the same way: there is a branch manager, and two counter assistants. The only exception to this pattern is the Head Office, which carries a larger staff.

Young Savers campaign

Roland Hayday has become anxious that the Society's image is a little stale in the communities it serves. He therefore decides to hold a campaign in all branches that will have two aims:

1   To publicise the Society effectively.
2   To bring in new savers, boosting the client lists in preparation for the projected opening of new offices.

He resolves on a 'Young Savers' campaign, modelled on the similar campaigns conducted by the larger, nationally active building societies. There are two factors that cause Hayday to want a speedy implementation of this programme:

1   The Society is in danger of being eclipsed by its main rival in the region, the Central Western Building Society, who are of similar size

but advertise more heavily and are attracting a higher proportion of new borrowers than Householder.

2   The Board of Directors have agreed to launch the branch expansion quickly, in view of the competitive climate in the industry. They therefore require from Hayday a successful programme, to be launched at eight weeks' notice, and to run for fourteen weeks. Each branch will then submit figures on new borrowers, and the expansion plans will be made in detail by Head Office.

In view of the brief time-span available, Hayday decides to run the entire campaign himself, rather than employ a professional public relations and advertising consultancy. He spends a week of his time making plans and designing a programme and then summons all regional managers to an extraordinary meeting on Tuesday, 11 April 19XX. Unfortunately, because of illness, Mark Beale does not attend this meeting, but Hayday holds the meeting nonetheless.

The meeting is a small one; Hayday himself, Alison Wilks and Adrian Reid. Hayday introduces the idea and objectives of the 'Young Savers' campaign. He firmly believes in involving his subordinates in decision-making wherever possible, so he invites suggestions on particular promotional ideas, after introducing the project. Following a ninety-minute discussion, the following points are agreed:

1   The Young Savers campaign will begin in all branches on 18 June 19XX, and run for fourteen weeks.

2   Head Office will be responsible for the organisation of all leaflets and window bills, but each regional manager will have a promotional budget of £1400 to spend on local advertising in press, local radio or any other suitable medium.

3   The campaign will offer a building society account to anyone over the age of seven, and will allow the account holder to manage the account entirely independently once he/she reaches the age of fourteen.

4   Young savers will receive a pen and pencil set, colouring book and a special 'Householder holdall' with the company logo when they join. They will also receive birthday cards and be invited to tour the branch office on their birthday, accompanied by a parent if under fourteen.

Hayday is particularly keen on the last point, as he feels it may well draw new adult borrowers into the Society.

Following the meeting, Hayday departs in some haste for London, where he has a number of afternoon appointments, and where he hopes to organise a supplier for the gifts that will be used for the campaign.

As the meeting was a small one, Hayday did not take an official record in the form of minutes, but simply asked his secretary to take notes. After the meeting finishes and the regional managers have dispersed, the following conversation takes place:

HAYDAY: Right Jean, I've got to rush for that London train. Were you quite clear about those four points?

JEAN: Oh yes, Mr Hayday, everything is quite straightforward.

HAYDAY: Good. Please send a memo to Mark Beale itemising the points, and tell him to get going on it now. I'll see him when he's here next month – that's 14 May, isn't it? We'll discuss any details then. Thanks . . .

The following memo is sent to Mark Beale:

 Householder Building Society

MEMO

To   Mark Beale

From   Roland Hayday

Date   11 April 198X

YOUNG SAVERS CAMPAIGN

Please note the following four points, which are vital for your attention if we are to get a good start to this campaign on 15 June.

1   You will have a budget of £1400 for promotions.

2   The campaign is to get anyone over seven to open an account, but we are even more keen to attract their parents into branches.

3   All young savers will receive a pen/pencil set, holdall (Society colours and logo), birthday cards and a birthday tour of Head Office.

4   Head Office will supply you with all leaflets and window bills you will need.

Jean Guest

pp Roland Hayday

When Mark Beale arrives at Head Office on 14 May, he informs Hayday that he has ordered, collected and paid for a supply of 200 holdalls from a sports shop in Salisbury. This has cost £1000 from his budget, so he is still looking for an inexpensive supplier of pen and pencil sets.

The Branch Manager at Salisbury has allowed one of his counter assistants to organise birthday tours, and she has opened a diary for this purpose. Two young children have already indicated their interest, and their parents have been into the office – in a state of some irritation – to enquire, 'What is the Building Society doing whisking our children off to Winchester? Let's have some official details.' One of the parents, Mr James Davenport, is the Headmaster of a local junior school and a frequent writer of letters to the town's local newspaper. The Branch Manager has approached Beale for details and help before replying.

Planning and solving

By this time, you should have a firm sense of the operations of Householder Building Society, and of its particular problems in its 'Young Savers' campaign.

The next stage is, therefore, to plan some possible solutions to the problems raised and revealed by the case, and to select the best of the possible solutions.

Having considered the case and worked through the 'Analysis' section on page 1, now consider each of the following issues:

- What is to be accomplished overall? In specific terms:
- What is to be corrected?
- What is to be improved?
- What is to be eliminated?

Make a list of these considerations, and rank your list in order of importance.

Having done this, propose a solution which will deal with each of the issues you have identified in the opening part of your 'Planning and solving' activity.

Exercises

The exercises that follow may be attempted individually or as an integrated group.

1   Produce an organisation chart showing the organisation of Householder Building Society. Include a series of footnotes that explain at which point in the organisation each breakdown in communication took place.

2 Produce a *Diagnostic report* for the Board of Directors on the problems surrounding the 'Young Savers' campaign.
3 Produce a discussion document for the Board of Directors that lays a foundation for discussion on
    (a) Advantages/disadvantages of adhering to 'Young Savers' campaign.
    (b) Benefits/drawbacks of scrapping the campaign.
    (c) Range of adjustments that appear available.
    (d) Implications of each adjustment for campaign, and existing practices.
4 Write a letter of conciliation/explanation to Mr James Davenport, 15 Druid Street, Salisbury, Wiltshire.

Notes for students

Answer guidelines

These guidelines accompany only the first case study, and offer suggestions for suitable approaches to the exercises.

Organisation chart · The chart should clearly differentiate the branches and management structure of the Society. It should be uncluttered, easy to read and visually inviting. Footnotes should detail the breakdown of the communication process, and the footnotes should relate to numbers, located (perhaps in a distinctive ink colour) on the chart itself, to show the point of communication breakdown.

Diagnostic report · The diagnostic report should have the following sections:

- Terms of reference: to identify and comment on the problems that have accompanied the 'Young Savers' campaign.
- Procedure: a section explaining how the information was researched and assembled.
- Findings: the main body of the report.
- Conclusions: that there have been significant difficulties with the campaign. A brief summary of how these arose.

Discussion document · A concise document, in the form of numbered points, using headings and subheadings, raising the following points:

    (a) Advantages/disadvantages of adhering to the Young Savers campaign.
    (b) Benefits/drawbacks of scrapping the scheme.
    (c) Range of adjustements that appear possible.
    (d) Implications of each adjustment for campaign, and for existing practices.

Letter of conciliation · This should explain the Society's position, and justify the campaign overall, without admission of failure or misjudgement. Tone should be positive but not aggressive or unresponsive.

The tone should move to a mildly apologetic and reassuring one over the specific issue of lack of detailed explanation at Salisbury. The letter should not ascribe blame nor accept fault on the part of anyone within the Society, but should conciliate and apologise. Finally, it should lay a foundation for the possibility of future business with the complainant.

2 · The French Connection

This case study is designed to exercise the following areas:

1 Ability to identify and distinguish failures caused by the overall structure of the organisation.
2 Ability to detect difficulties caused by a particular management style.
3 Ability to detect the psychological and interpersonal factors that can influence successful communication in the workplace.
4 Appreciation of the influence of the working environment as a determinant of quality of internal communications.
5 Appreciation of the importance of tone management in dealing with customer relations.
6 Appreciation of factors of layout in brochure design and presentation.
7 Ability to conduct research into documents using the resources of a local or college library (Trade Descriptions Act).
8 Ability to tactfully point out areas of weakness and failure to a responsible executive.
9 Ability to write a diagnostic report.

Analytical skills

1 Ability to detect, distinguish and rank the causes of a problem.
2 Ability to distinguish local and general failures in organisation/communication.
3 Ability to interpret legislation (Trade Descriptions Act) in the context of a particular case.

Introduction

Francetour is a company operating in the UK from a single office near Victoria station. Its sole activity is to market and administer holidays from the UK to France, and it specialises particularly in Paris, where it sells over 25 000 holidays per year, from weekend breaks to holidays of a fortnight or more.

The marketing activities of Francetour are relatively small; it produces a holiday brochure annually, which is distributed by all major travel agents. It also produces posters for outlets such as railway stations, shopping centres and travel agents.

The staff of Francetour numbers twenty-seven, all of whom are located at the one London office. The Managing Director, M. Patrick Desfours, is a Frenchman aged fifty, who speaks perfect English as a result of spending his career with 'Leiseurope', a large international conglomerate that runs a number of holiday and entertainment companies throughout Europe, including a ski complex in Austria, a chain of sub-aqua and sailing training centres in Yugoslavia, and a number of casinos in France and Monte Carlo. As the language of business throughout Leiseurope is English, M. Desfour's twenty-seven years with the group have served him well. Leiseurope is the holiday company of Francetour, and is located in offices in Paris. M. Desfours is an employee of Leiseurope and an executive director of the company, which requires him to spend a large proportion of his time in Paris, where he frequently has to go at short notice.

The remaining twenty-six employees at Francetour, London, are all employees of Francetour, and are all UK nationals. The majority of jobs are clerical and secretarial, although there is one manager of marketing and public relations, Mr Derek Mainwell and one manager of administration and contracts, Mr Bernard Cavendish. Cavendish is a graduate in law, and aged twenty-six. He joined Francetour after a period of unemployment following his graduation. Bernard had hoped to enter a solicitor's office, but found no vacancy, so he joined Francetour initially as a clerk, and was promoted after seven months to the position of Administration Manager. His promotion was unexpected, as many employees at Francetour have remained in a clerical capacity for periods as long as twelve years.

The staff at Francetour have been advised that, due to computerisation of bookings, it will need to shed eight staff members within a period of fifteen months. All job losses will be at clerical level.

In the current year, the company has, at the suggestion of Derek Mainwell, introduced a series of specialised package weekends to Paris, including the 'Treasures of Art' weekend, involving a tour of the Louvre Art Gallery, and a special weekend trip for honeymooners, called the 'Just Married Special'. These have been successful and are recognised by Leiseurope as a welcome marketing initiative, especially as Francetour had been selling fewer holidays for each of the preceding two years.

On Tuesday, 16 May the following letter arrives at Francetour, and is passed to Derek Mainwell's tray for action:

---

56 Brace Drive
Dartford
Kent

12 May 198X

Managing Director
Francetour
Zenith House
Victoria
London SW1

Dear Sir

I write following our return on Monday from a 'Just Married Special' organized by your company, which was a wedding present to my wife and me from my wife's father, Mr David Metherell. I knew little about the trip before we actually departed, but would make the following points as you are the organizer of the holiday:

1 You advertise travel to Paris by 'mid morning service'. In fact, when we arrived at Victoria station, we found that our train (the 11.00) had been cancelled and we eventually travelled on the 13.00. Hardly mid morning service.

2 On arrival at the railway station in Paris, your guide did indeed meet us, and sent us by taxi to our hotel - the one smooth part of the operation. On arriving at the hotel, we were told that our room would be unavailable until 20.00, as the hotel was being recarpeted and our room was currently being done. We therefore left our cases at Reception and, without the benefit of a bath or a change of clothes, went out to dinner.

3 On returning from dinner we did gain access to our room, where we found the following:

(a) Twin beds - hardly appropriate in the circumstances.
(b) Instead of the bottle of champagne that your brochure advertised, we found only a one-litre bottle of mineral water.
(c) There were no flowers in the room, only an ageing pot plant which had also done recent service as an ashtray.
(d) When I pointed out (a), (b) and (c) to the proprietor, he informed me that his was only a two-star hotel, and that it was necessary to live with a sense of humour.

-2-

He also explained that it was against the rules of the
hotel to move furniture, and that all beds were screwed
to the floor. This is true.

The remainder of the 'holiday' passed off uneventfully.

It appears to me that Francetour has failed to sell me
a holiday similar to the one advertised, and that therefore there is a breach of the Trades Descriptions Act.
Would you please be kind enough to give me your views in
writing on the above matters. I would comment that I
would be prepared to drop the matter if you refunded
25% of the total outlay of Mr Metherell, i.e. £75.00
(25% of £300.00).

I look forward to hearing from you.

Yours sincerely

JVBarnes

J V Barnes

Derek Mainwell is on holiday for two weeks from Monday, 15 May. On Thursday, 18 May, one of the clerical staff noted the growing pile of mail for Mainwell, and, on drawing this to the attention of M. Desfours, she is advised to open and sort the mail into two piles: 'Priority' (to be handled before his return) and 'Non Priority' (to await his return). The letter from Mr Barnes is the only one to be categorised as 'Priority' and so the clerical worker, Sonia Whitehorne, takes it in to M. Desfours.

M. Desfours is irritated by this, as he had just received a telex from Leiseurope instructing him that he must be in Paris by five o'clock that afternoon for an urgent board meeting. The following conversation takes place:

SONIA: M. Desfours, I think you should look at this letter for Mr Mainwell.

M. DESFOURS: I'm so sorry, Sonia, I'm rushing to Heathrow. Can you handle it for me, whatever it is?

SONIA: Oh, I don't think so! I'm really only a typist, M. Desfours.

M. DESFOURS: I really don't have time to look at it now, and I may be tied up in Paris for a couple of days. Would you be very kind and pass it round to anyone you think might handle it, with my permission to go ahead? Thanks.

SONIA: But Mr Mainwell always handles complaints, and he's away for two weeks!

M. DESFOURS: Yes, I know, but I really must go. Do your best, and I'll take responsibility. Thanks. Sorry, I have to rush.

Sonia is left with the problem of the letter. As she has a lot of work to do, she passes it direct to Donald Burton, a clerk in his late forties who has worked at Francetour for sixteen years. On reading the letter, he says, 'Oh that bright spark Cavendish knows all about the law. I'll give it to him.'

Donald Burton does this. However, he ignores the opportunity to explain what Sonia has told him of the background to events and simply marks the letter 'Attention B. Cavendish', and places it in the mail tray that Bernard shares with two other staff.

Consequently, it is 22 May before Bernard finds the letter and attends to it. As it is marked for his attention he assumes that M. Desfours has seen it and drafts a reply based *only* on the legal situation, governed by the Francetour charter and Trade Descriptions Act. He is not experienced in public relations and so writes rather a brief and official letter.

On 24 May, Mr Barnes arrives at the office, angrily demanding a meeting with the Managing Director, who is still in Paris . . .

Analysis

Read the case study carefully and then attempt the following, individually or in discussion:

1   How far was Francetour responsible for the problems of Mr and Mrs Barnes?

2   In what way did each of the following factors contribute to the problem:

(a) The management style of Desfours.
(b) The way Francetour was organised internally.
(c) The relationship between Francetour and the holding company and the resultant staffing.
(d) The working environment at Francetour.
(e) The interpersonal factors in the office at Francetour.

Planning and solving

Having considered the case, consider each of the following:

- What is to be accomplished overall?
- What is to be corrected?
- What is to be improved?
- What is to be eliminated?

Make a list of these considerations.

Rank them in order of importance.

Categorise them according to whether they can be accomplished short-term or long-term.

Having done this, propose a solution for each of the issues raised in 'Planning and solving'.

After each proposed solution, note 'possible drawbacks' of the solution in question.

---

3. If we change or cancel your holiday or arrangements

It is unlikely we shall have to change your holiday. But we must reserve the right to do so, if necessary.

3a. Minor changes

Sometimes we need to make minor changes, and we will let you know about these as soon as possible. Please remember that, too, whilst this brochure is based on recent inspections and information obtained from the locality, hotels and other locations sometimes do withdraw or alter facilities. The timings of train, ship and air travel, although correct at time of going to press, can be subject to alterations by various organisations, companies or authorities or for operational reasons. You must adhere to the timings shown on your final documents.

3b. Major changes

A major change is one involving a change in resort area, or a change of hotel to one with a lower star rating but not a change in mode of travel or itinerary. It does not cover travel delays or changes forced on us by events beyond our control (see 3c below).

3c. Important note

No compensation payments apply if there are any changes or cancellations made due to war or threat of war, riots, civil strife, industrial action, natural disaster, epidemics, bad weather, technical problems with aircraft or other transport and airports, closure of ports and airports, terrorist activity, governmental action or other events where our ability to carry out our promise is frustrated or made significantly more difficult by events beyond our control. If a major change or cancellation takes place within thirty five days of the date of departure FC will endeavour to offer you an alternative FC holiday of at least comparable standard if available, or alternatively a refund of all money paid less a deduction in respect of all costs and expenses that FC have incurred.

3d. Major change procedure

We hope that a major change will not become necessary. If it does, then subject to paragraph 3c above, we will notify you in writing and you may accept it with the compensation shown in 3e below or choose any comparable alternative we can offer. If you prefer, then subject as above, you may cancel altogether, provided that you notify us in writing within ten days of our notification; in this case, we will refund all the money you have paid.

3e. Compensation for major changes
Unless the reason for the major change as listed in 3c above, we will compensate you for major changes (if you go ahead with the altered holidays) as follows: Period before scheduled departure within which a major change is notified to you:

	Compensation per person		
More than 42 days	29–42 days	15–28 days	0–14 days
Nil	£10	£15	£20

Exercises

The exercises that follow may be taken singly or as an integrated group.

1 Use a local library to research the Trade Description Act. Which section/sections would Mr Barnes be likely to use, should he decide to prosecute Francetour?
   Which sections of the Act could Francetour use in its defence?
2 Prepare a report for M. Desfours on the entire story. Include your conclusions and recommendations.
3 Draft a letter to Mr Barnes to be sent after his visit to the office.
4 Draft a footnote for possible inclusion in the brochure to prevent a similar problem in future.
5 Produce a discussion paper for the directors of Leiseurope, of a maximum 420 words, in which you summarise the events and point out weaknesses in organisation and staffing of Francetour.
6 Develop a draft *Code of Practice* for handling complaints at Francetour (in discussion group).

Note: The relevant sections of the Trade Descriptions Act (1968) are as follows:

1 Section 9, paragraph 3.
2 Sections 13 and 14.
3 Section 24 (Defences).

You may also like to consult Chapter 10 of *A Guide to Consumer Protection Law* by A.A. Painter, published by Barry Rose.

3 · Stainton and Wrigland Ltd

This case study will involve the exercise of the following skills:

1 Conducting of independent research.
2 Writing a memo.
3 Analysing a telephone conversation in terms of the efficiency of both the initiator and the recipient of the call.
4 Analysing discourse in terms of efficiency and tone.
5 Discussing the suitability of the telephone for a particular type of message.
6 Participation in a group discussion that arrives at definite conclusions as a result of interpretation, evaluation and hypothesis.
7 Contribution to an oral presentation in which both causes and possible solutions to the problem are advanced.

Introduction

Stainton and Wrigland is a small partnership that was established in 1981. It is situated in modern premises, consisting of a workshop/production area and goods yard, and an office for sales and executive staff, on a new industrial estate on the outskirts of Rochdale, Lancashire. The company has only one product, a high quality and expensive drinks vending machine, the 'Stainland Hostess'.

The machine is expensive because it is designed as a departure from the normal type of vending machine usually found in offices and factories. Matthew Stainton, the designer of the machine and Managing Director of the company, produced it after using a number of vending machines in his working life, and frequently having cause to complain about them, most usually about very poor quality drinks, due to aged ingredients, the unpleasantness of thin plastic cups that allow hot liquids to burn the fingers and the use of powdered milk.

Matthew had spent his entire working life (thirty-one years) as an electrical engineer in the Sheffield area, firstly with a manufacturer of radios, and then with a washing machine company. When the company closed in 1980, he was made redundant (at the age of forty-six), as was his lifelong friend Norman Wrigland, who had been one of the sales managers for the company.

Matthew and Norman put their redundancy money, plus a bank

loan and a grant for small businesses from the Department of Employment, into the formation of Stainton and Wrigland, the company that developed the Hostess.

The Hostess is unusual amongst vending machines for a number of reasons. While it operates according to the standard principles of such machines, it boasts a number of refinements that should, in the view of both partners, make it very popular. Firstly, it makes coffee by actually grinding the coffee beans within the machine as a drink is ordered, thus ensuring excellent flavour. Tea is kept in a vacuum cylinder and so is similarly fresh. Two other major refinements are that the machine uses fresh milk and is designed to dispense drinks in china mugs rather than plastic cups. All these features increase unit costs, so that a cup of tea or coffee is likely to cost 30 per cent more than from standard vending machines, but Matthew and Norman both feel that the design should prove very popular in pubs, offices, hotels, hospitals and leisure centres.

The company employs five people in addition to the two director-partnerships; one secretary/executive assistant, one driver and delivery man, and three assemblers who build the machines from components delivered to the workshop by various suppliers.

Matthew controls all production work and Norman organises marketing. He soon finds that he needs a deputy, so they appoint Wayne Tyson, one of Norman's neighbours, as a sales executive.

Wayne left the local technical college aged nineteen with a BTEC diploma, and has since worked as a salesman with a large insurance company, Eagle Crest.

When making previous appointments, Matthew and Norman had initially written a job description, advertised in a local newspaper and at the job centre, interviewed the candidates together and checked references carefully before making an offer of employment.

In the case of Wayne, this was not done. References were not taken up as Norman had known Wayne since Wayne's birth and no advertisement was taken. Wayne had, in fact, been recommended by his father, George Tyson, who said that Wayne was dissatisfied with the lack of recognition for his efforts in a big company and wanted to move.

Additionally, no job description was drafted for Wayne, as it was agreed that he would be 'working under Norman'. Wayne was equipped with a small van for demonstrations and told to 'develop the business' with a programme of calls from sales leads provided by Norman.

After the first month of Wayne's employment, Norman was dissatisfied. Wayne had brought in only three orders (one of which had been promised prior to Wayne's employment). Additionally,

Norman felt that Wayne kept poor records of sales calls and van mileage, and strongly suspected that he was cheating the firm over petrol expenses. Norman was particularly annoyed when, one Friday evening, he visited a favourite pub, run by a personal friend, who told him that Wayne had made the briefest of sales calls at the pub earlier that week and had spent only ten minutes demonstrating and discussing the Hostess, but had then spent an hour and fifteen minutes on a bar lunch in the pub, chatting to the barmaid. Slightly incensed by this news, Norman immediately telephoned Wayne at home from the pub.

NW: Good evening. Can I speak to Wayne Tyson, please?

WT: Speaking!

NW: Ah, Wayne, just the lad I want a word with. I'm speaking from the Joiners' Arms at Brighthouse, where the landlord, Ted Parker, says you called yesterday.

WT: Yes, that's right. Quite a coincidence really, Mr Wrigland, because I'm coming out there myself tonight; just about to leave actually.

NW: What? In the firm's van?

WT: Er, no. On my motor bike.

NW: Right, well, never mind that now. Ted here tells me you only spent ten minutes here on Tuesday and hardly showed him the machine. Is that true?

WT: No, I spent a lot longer there. I know I did, because I stayed for lunch.

NW: But how long did you spend showing the machine?

WT: Couldn't say exactly. But could all this wait until Monday, Mr Wrigland, because I've got my girl friend here with her coat on and we're ready to go out.

NW: Now look, Wayne, this is important. You haven't brought in good results this month and we're not a big enough firm to carry people who don't produce the goods.

WT: Uh, well, I must say a salesman's only as good as his product and his leads, you know. When I was at Eagle Crest I was salesman of the month twice, and I was the youngest ever to win it.

NW: Eagle Crest was a big company with an established reputation. A salesman with a new outfit has to work hard; he can't ride on his company's name.

WT: *I do work hard!* Have you seen how many calls I made last week?

NW: No, I haven,t because you haven't put your sales report in for the last two weeks – nor your mileage figures either. Who paid for the petrol in your motor bike?

WT: I'm not sure what you're saying, Mr Wrigland.

NW: Never mind that now. Look, I think that what I want you to understand is that Stainton and Wrigland is a small company struggling to make an impact and get on top of the competition.

WT: Well, you're right about the competition. Half the people tell me they can rent or buy a machine at half the price and sometimes get commission on drinks sold.

NW: It's your job to *overcome* objections like that – that's how a salesman makes a sale.

WT: My girl friend's waiting, Mr Wrigland, and it's eight o'clock on Friday night.

NW: If you want to work for me, lad, you have to listen whenever I talk to you. And this girl – she's not the lunchtime assistant at the Joiners' Arms, I suppose?

WT: I really don't think that's the firm's business, Mr Wrigland.

NW: Were you talking to her all Tuesday lunchtime?

WT: I'm afraid I don't think it's company business, Mr Wrigland. Now, if you've finished, I'll look forward to seeing you on Mon –

NW: I've not finished. I'm far from finished. Let's see you tomorrow morning, eight o'clock in the office.

WT: I don't work Saturdays.

NW: You come in tomorrow. I want to go over your sales methods. I don't think you're making enough of the product advantages, and we'll have to work on that. Come in tomorrow, nine o'clock.

WT: I can't, I'm away for the weekend. I think the product has got advantages, yes, but it's also got a big fat price, and no commission for operators, but that's what's killing us, to my mind.

NW: I'm the Sales Director and I'll set the prices. You be there at nine!

WT: I'm going away, Mr Wrigland, and that's settled long ago. I never have worked Saturdays.

NW: If you don't come in tomorrow, you'd best not come in at all.

WT: Ever heard of unfair dismissal? You'd lose your small firm's grant then. I know I'm not in the wrong.

Norman Wrigland puts the telephone down without continuing the conversation. Frustrated and angry, he returns home to Rochdale. The following morning, he goes into the works, but Wayne does not arrive.

Stil more annoyed, Norman explains the whole story to his secretary who he then instructs to research the Employment Protection Act and to let him know the legislation about *unfair dismissal* and *constructive dismissal* might affect this case.

He also drafts an advertisement for the local newspaper for a sales representative . . .

Analysis

1   List all the primary causes of the problem.

2   Divide these into *organisational* causes (causes that arose through weaknesses in the policy or operations of the organisation as a whole) and *personal/attitudinal* causes (causes that arose through the attitudes or behaviour of the individuals concerned).

3   Identify any secondary causes of the communication problem between Norman Wrigland and Wayne Tyson. (A secondary cause is a cause that arises because of the existence of an earlier, or *primary* cause).

4   Identify the effects of each primary cause (include any secondary causes in your list of effects.

Planning and solving

Begin by determining your overall aim in dealing with the case:

- What needs to be accomplished?

Once this is established, go on to consider the following:

- What needs to be eliminated?
- What needs to be improved?
- What needs to be corrected?

Exercises

1   Conduct an analysis of the personal and organisational problems of the company, exclusively from the viewpoint of Wayne Tyson.

2   Conduct an analysis of the personal and organisational weaknesses of the company, exclusively from the viewpoint of Norman Wrigland.

3   In a group of at least three, conduct a role play exercise as follows:

Matthew Stainton hears of the conversation between Norman and Wayne and requests a 'discussion' with both of them over the issue of company sales strategy, to be held in his office on the following Monday at 2 p.m.

Select three people to play the roles of Stainton, Wrigland and Tyson and discuss the resultant outcome of the role play. See the glossary for notes on role play.

4   Using your college or public library, conduct the research that Norman Wrigland requests, using the Employment Protection Act. Research both *unfair dismissal* and *constructive dismissal*. The Department of Employment leaflet 'Unfairly Dismissed?', available from Job Centres, will be helpful.

5   Prepare a memo report for Mr Wrigland that summarises the above points of the Employment Protection Act and provides any relevant information to Stainton and Wrigland. In particular, is it true that the firm may lose out financially if it is found guilty of the unfair dismissal of Wayne Tyson?

6 Prepare a critical report on the telephone conversation between Norman Wrigland and Wayne Tyson in which you consider the following:

(a) The suitability (or otherwise) of the telephone as a medium for this particular message.
(b) The qualities and shortcomings of Wrigland's telephone usage.
(c) The qualities and shortcomings of Tyson's telephone usage.
(d) The control and variation of *tone* of each of them during the conversation.
(e) Identify the following:

  (i) Points in the conversation where there was significant communication and transaction (i.e. the listener reacting in the way that the speaker intends) during the conversation.
  (ii) Points in the conversation where there was a failure in transaction (i.e. the listener failed to react in the way intended by the speaker, or reacted in a quite different way).
  (iii) Points in the conversation where there was almost, or entirely, no communication between the two participants.
  (iv) Reasons for the breakdown mentioned in (iii) above.

7 Discuss in groups the likely outcome of each of the following courses:

(a) Dismissing Wayne.
(b) Keeping Wayne and making no further changes.
(c) Keeping Wayne and changing pricing structure of product.
(d) Keeping Wayne after a warning on his conduct.
(e) Retraining Wayne.

Elect a spokesperson who explains the group's views on the above issues to the remainder of the class in an oral presentation. (See note on oral presentation.)

8 List what you think the company needs to do in order to make Wayne (or his replacement) a more effective sales executive.

A note on oral presentation

An oral presentation may take many forms. It may be as simple as a brief summary of a small business discussion or event passed on in speech to some working colleagues, or it may take the form of a considered and prepared speech, delivered within the context of a formal meeting or social function.

The presentation may be entirely your own work, or it may be the work of a number of people for whom you act as spokesperson. Whatever its precise nature, the following principles are likely to improve it:

Preparation

1   Compose an outline of what you want to say. This will consist of a few main headings, rearranged in order, so that you retain a firm idea of the structure and progress of your talk as it proceeds.
2   Consider whether any visual aids will help the clarity and effectiveness of what you say. Diagrams, graphs, bar and pie charts, or even a simple list of principal points for an audience to follow, can all support your presence and create an added sense of impact.
3   Pre-consider audience response: try to anticipate the audience's particular interest in your topic, their likely concentration span (an issue that will influence the length of your presentation), and any questions or feedback you are likely to gain.
4   Remember the principle – 'Say what you're going to say; say it; then say you've said it.'

In other words, when preparing include a brief *introduction*, in which you outline the main contents before you develop them in the mid-section of your presentation. When you have done the latter, summarise briefly as a *conclusion*.

Delivery

1   Make sure that you are happy with your appearance. Dress in a way that makes you feel relaxed, yet confident and smart. (This issue does not, of course, arise if you are making the presentation within your normal day-to-day work.)
2   Concentrate on addressing all of the audience by transferring your glance to different places.
3   Start positively (with adequate volume and reasonable pace) and adjust later, according to your sense of the audience.
4   Do be conscious of your speaking speed – nervousness tends to increase normal speaking speed and it is often useful deliberately to speak slightly more slowly than usual.

Employment legislation – research material

1   Department of Employment pamphlet PL 716, 'Individual Rights of Employees'.
2   Department of Employment pamphlet No. 13, 'Unfairly Dismissed?'.
3   Reasons for Dismissal, Section D SS, *Employment Law*, Croner Publications.
4   Employment Protection Act (1978), HMSO:
    (a) (Sections 54–55), Meaning of Dismissal.
    (b) Section 57, General Provisions Relating to Dismissal.

4 · Automation at Midwest

This case study involves the following skills:

1 Discussion and analysis of dialogue.
2 Production of a notice.
3 Skills in research and information retrieval on a given topic.
4 Synthesis of material from a variety of externally researched sources into one document.
5 The drafting of a letter of evidence to an independent external body.
6 The writing of a letter of conciliation.
7 Adjustment of message and message style to meet the tastes of the receiver.
8 Identification and application of the principles relating to dialogue.

Introduction

The Midwest Bank is one of the largest clearing banks in the UK, with over 1500 branches, many of which are in city centre and high street sites, in order to meet the heavy demand for retail banking transactions. The branch at Tipmarket, Suffolk, is no exception. Situated in the main shopping street of a provincial market and light industrial town, which has a population of 42 000, the bank employs a total staff of twelve full-time officers.

The most senior of these are Haydn Temple and James Arnold, managers of the branch. Temple is aged forty-seven, was born in nearby Cambridge, and has worked within the East Anglia region of the bank throughout his working life. James Arnold, however, is thirty-one years old and is in his first managerial position, having graduated in Banking and Financial Studies from the University of Manchester eight years previously, the date at which he joined the bank as a management trainee.

Tipmarket is seen as an important branch by the bank's East Anglia regional office at Cambridge. There are two reasons for this: firstly, the area holds a number of wealthy farmers who use the town as a banking centre, not only for cash transactions, but also for investments and securities, an aspect of activity that the regional office is very eager to develop. For this reason, another recent graduate, thirty-year-old Malcolm Ellers, has recently been transferred from one of the bank's large City of London offices in order to become Head of Securities at Tipmarket. However, in view of his youth, Malcolm spends one day each week at Head Office in London studying investment analysis with the senior Securities Manager there.

The second reason for the importance of the Tipmarket branch is the growth of a number of new high technology industries in the region, many of which have been attracted by the excellent new road links to London, the low cost of land, and the attractiveness of the East Anglia region. This influx of firms, mainly in the computer and domestic appliance industries, has given another significant boost to the level of business at Midwest, Tipmarket.

However, the bank does have some problems. Tipmarket is traditionally a small and stable farming community, and this is reflected in the very low turnover of staff at the bank, especially at cashier level, where four of the five cashiers are married ladies over the age of fifty who have lived in the town all their lives, and who have no intention of moving. This means that they are reluctant to go on courses organised by the bank, as they have no interest in promotion or job mobility. It is, therefore, difficult for Haydn Temple to keep his staff abreast of the rapid range of change in retail banking procedures, a problem that greatly concerns him, but to which he has no clear solution.

This problem has been emphasised by the recent introduction of the 'Autobanker' computerised cash and service dispenser, which is mounted on the outside wall of the bank and which replaces the old night safe system. The new machine can issue cash and bank statements, and can also accept deposits in cash and cheque form. As such deposits are made in envelopes 22 cm × 11 cm, it is technically possible for clients to write instructions to the bank when depositing their funds, although the bank does not officially encourage or even publicly recognise this practice.

Aside from Arnold, Temple and Ellers, the bank has three qualified accountants, one of whom specialises in foreign transactions. There is also a secretary (Norma Mann), a chief cashier, Ellen Stout, and four cashiers.

Ella Stout's responsibility includes monitoring the level of cash stocks in the bank, and supervising the Autobanker. In the event of a breakdown of the system, a maintenance engineer from Cambridge has to be called in. Cambridge is forty miles from Tipmarket.

Ella herself is uneasy about her work. She realises that the staff she supervises are not well motivated, largely because, like her, they are approaching retirement. She has attempted to persuade them to go on training courses, but has not persisted after encountering initial objections. She confides this difficulty to Haydn Temple, who agrees to 'think it over'. However, as Temple is the brother-in-law of one of the diffident cashiers, and a close personal friend of another, he is, himself, reluctant to act firmly.

Two regular customers of the bank are Simon Deeley, Company Treasurer of Amstead, a computer assembly factory on the outskirts of town, and Andrew Mossop, an extremely successful and wealthy local farmer and landowner, who runs a number of racehorses, and who also deposits large amounts of funds with the bank for placement in securities.

The following is an account of two days in Tipmarket in August 198X . . .

Friday, 10 August 198X.
Haydn Temple spends the day preparing to take his fortnight's summer holiday, which is to begin the following Monday. He clears up as much outstanding business as he can, checks that there are no new items of business likely to occur during his holiday period, and briefs James Arnold on the operations to be followed during his absence. He suggests that Arnold, as a younger man, new to the area, might be successful in selling the idea of a training course to be held at regional office, Cambridge, for Ella Stout and the other tellers. He particularly had in mind a two-day course, 'Modern High Street Banking Techniques', which includes a lot of work on automated banking. Arnold agrees to try to secure the cashiers' acceptance to going on the course.

Malcolm Ellers seeks a brief interview with Arnold. As it is August and many of Tipmarket's wealthier clients are away on holiday, investment business is very slow. Arnold, therefore, agrees to Ellers' requests to spend two days of the following week in London, rather than the usual one.

At the Amstead offices, Simon Deeley receives a telex informing him that a Japanese cargo ship, the *Hokkaido*, due to dock at Felixstowe on Monday, 13 August is carrying a cargo of semi-conductors for Amstead that must be paid for in cash, owing to a delay in issuing documentary credits in Japan. There is a 20 per cent discount on the price of £16 000 if cash is paid to the ship's purser at Felixstowe on 13 August, prior to its departure for Rotterdam on the evening tide at 6 p.m.

```
86-12-09   15:09
Msg 402 Title:


534290 PITMAN G
32591  BXNTER G

4594 10 AUGUST 198X

TO:   SIMON DEELEY
      COMPANY TREASURER
      AMSTEAD, TIPMARKET, SUFFOLK

FROM: LISSAN SHIPPING CO.,
      TOKYO

SEMI-CONDUCTORS ON SHIP 'HOKKAIDO' ARRIVING FELIXSTOWE 13 AUGUST
198X.  DOCUMENTARY CREDITS DELAY HERE MEANS PAYMENT MUST BE CASH.
20% DISCOUNT ON £16,000 PRICE IF CASH PAID TO PURSER ON 13 AUGUST
BEFORE SHIP SAILS TO ROTTERDAM ON EVENING TIDE 1800 HOURS.

534290 PITMAN G
32591 BXNTER G
```

At 4 p.m. in the afternoon, Andrew Mossop, while talking to a friend on the telephone, is strongly advised to invest £8000 in some shares that will be available for sale in London from the following Monday. As they are likely to be popular, Mossop descides to buy on the Monday morning, to guard against a price rise. When he drives through Tipmarket at 7 p.m., he places instructions to Malcolm Ellers to effect the transaction through the bank. These instructions are in the form of a letter than he posts into the Autobanker machine. Mossop has folded it carelessly, and the machine jams. Of the 117 people who try to get cash from the Autobanker over the weekend, not one is successful . . .

Monday, 13 August 198X.
Ella Stout and the tellers arrive at the bank shortly after James Arnold, at 8.50 a.m. They see the notice (on page 28) on the bank's personnel notice board.

The three cashiers, all of whom have at least eight years' service with the bank are shocked and irritated by the notice. Their anger is not helped by the steady stream of customers complaining of the Autobanker failure over the weekend. When Temple suggests telephoning the maintenance section in Cambridge, one of the cashiers replies to him, 'I'm surprised you think I can use a telephone properly. Do it yourself if you're so clever.'

Temple then spends fifteen minutes on the telephone to Cambridge,

13 August 198X

On Thursday and Friday, 23/24 August, Regional Office

in Cambridge is running a two-day course, 'Modern High

Street Banking Techniques'.

The following will attend on behalf of this branch:

Ella Stout plus all cashiers.

Accommodation at Crest Hotel, Cambridge, at the

expense of the bank. Please confirm your availability

by 10 a.m., 14 August, to me.

No banker, however minor his or her job, can stand

still in today's world! It is part of our obligation

to the people of Tipmarket to keep up with developments.

Best of luck.

J Arnold

trying to secure an appointment with the engineer. He is, therefore, late for an appointment with Andrew Mossop, who, when he does enter, takes part in the following exchange:

AM: Morning. Let's be quick, please, as I'm busy. I need to see Ellers.

JT: I'm afraid he's away, Mr Mossop. He's spending two days in London this week, and I imagine he went down for a long weekend. He's got a girl friend there, you see.

AM: So who's handling my investment?

JT: Which investment, Mr Allsop?

AM: My £8000 share purchase, that's what. I instructed Ellers on Friday.

JT: Oh, I didn't know. If you instructed him, I'm sure he'll handle it.

AM: Yes, but it was written – a note. I put it through the Autobanker on Friday night.

JT: Oh, that's probably what jammed the wretched machine. It does need to be used with care, Mr Mossop.

AM: Never mind the machine, and don't you lecture a man twenty years your senior. Now, anyway, what about these shares?

JT: I'm very sorry, Mr Mossop. Malcolm's away and as it's Mr Arnold's holiday, I'm really the only manager there. I won't be able to help you with any securities business today – or tomorrow, for that matter. May I suggest you drive over to Cambridge.

AM: I've banked here for thirty years, and I've had a good service until today –

JT: I am sorry, Mr Mossop, but realistically it's your best chance of buying your shares, always assuming the offer hasn't been completely snapped up already. It's nearly 11.30 and those City brokers move fast, you know.

AM: I've had enough. You can't run your bank, then you insult the local people. I'll be driving to Cambridge today, but not to buy shares. I want to see the Regional Manager for Midwest, East Anglia, and I won't be back here until Temple's back; and maybe not then. Goodbye.

The day at the bank proceeds uneventfully until mid afternoon, although Temple notices that the staff are all very cool towards him. At 3 p.m. Simon Deeley enters the bank, accompanied by two security guards from Amstead. He approaches Ella Stout, with whom he has dealt on a number of previous visits. The following conversation takes place:

SD: Good afternoon, Mrs Stout. Simon Deeley of Amstead.

ES: Oh yes, Mr Deeley. Nice to see you again. How can we help? Your payroll delivery isn't until Thursday, is it?

SD: No, that's right. This is rather an unusual one. I need £12 800 in cash please, drawn on the company's current account.

ES: Yes . . . Er, does Mr Temple know?

SD: No, it's a straightforward one, though. Just debit the current account. Look, I hate to rush you, but we've got to get over to Felixstowe, so if you could process the payment . . .

ES: Just one moment, Mr Deeley. I'm afraid there's a problem. You really should have phoned first. You see our Autobanker broke down over the weekend.

SD: Yes, yes, I know you've got a lot of difficulties, but look, I've got to get to Felixstowe, so please hurry the payment.

ES: I don't think you understand the problem. So many people were short of money over the weekend that we've paid out much more than usual. We're very relieved it's closing time in ten minutes, because we've only £2150 left in cash. Can you imagine how embarrassing it would be if Tipmarket Midwest had to close its doors! We'd be in the papers, famous at last, Mr Deeley! Never mind about your money. If you come in tomorrow we'll have had an extra cash delivery from Cambr –

SD: I need the money *now*. Your failure to supply will mean a loss of discount of £3200.

ES: Well, we can't pay out what we haven't got, that's common sense, isn't it? We'd like to help, Mr Deeley, but I'm afraid there's nothing I can do. I can only issue what's there. There's not much there, so I can't issue much. I'm sorry, but we will help tomorrow.

SD: It is simple incompetence for a bank to be caught out like this. When did the Autobanker go wrong?

ES: Well, over the weekend. But I'm afraid it's not bank policy to discuss operations with outsiders, Mr Deeley, and if you'll excuse me, there is a line of people waiting . . .

SD: The manager. Where's the manager?

ES: He's in Corfu, on his holiday. Please excuse me, won't you?

SD: No one to answer, no one to deal with. My company will lose its discount. Right, Mrs Stout, we'll be submitting all this to your Head Office and claiming the lost discount from Midwest.

ES: I'm sorry, Mr Deeley, I'm with other customers now. I really am sorry . . .

After the close of business, Ella reports the incident to Arnold who starts to prepare a report on the incident for regional office.

Analysis

Consider the following points (you may like to produce answers individually, or in discussion groups):

1   Which of the problems of the bank were directly or indirectly caused by poor communication performance on the part of an individual?

2   Which of the problems can be ascribed to poor communication between the branch and regional headquarters?

3   Which failure in communication were partly or wholly caused by the staffing pattern and organisation of the branch and the resources devoted to management?

4   What was the primary cause of the breakdown in communication between the bank and Andrew Mossop and between the bank and Simon Deeley?

Planning and solving

What needs to be accomplished to make the Tipmarket branch an efficient and relaxed place of work with effective communication at all levels? In particular:

- What needs to be eliminated?
- What needs to be improved?
- What needs to be corrected?
- What needs to be strengthened?

Exercises

1   Comment on the level of communication skills shown in the dialogue between Temple and Mossop. To what extent do you consider either person a skilled or unskilled user of dialogue?

2   Comment on the success of Ella Stout's performance in dialogue with Simon Deeley. Consider her strengths and weaknesses and point out any shortcomings in the dialogue as a public relations exercise on behalf of the bank. (*Note*: You will find material on the nature of dialogue in the glossary, and a fuller account of this medium in Margaret Wolff and Graham Collins, *Communicating at Work*, Nelson, 1982.)

3   Evaluate the communicative skill of Arnold's notice, indicating the results that followed from the issuing of the notice.

4   *Either* re-write the notice in an improved form, *or* fully explain a more effective way of communicating this message by another medium, stressing the advantages of your chosen medium.

5   Write a letter of apology and conciliation to *either* Simon Deeley *or* Andrew Mossop, carefully controlling both content and tone according the particular recipient.

6   Present an information report for Haydn Temple on the events in the bank during his absence. Do not include recommendations.

7   Draft a letter of evidence on behalf of the Tipmarket branch to go to the Branch Supervision Director, Head Office, in defence of any complaint that may be made.

5 · Crisis at Comlon*

This chapter exercises the following skill areas:

1 Appreciation and analysis of the structure of organisations.
2 Appreciation of the relationship between organisational structure and the communication system of an organisation.
3 Appreciation and analysis of the physical and psychological barriers to effective communication.
4 Ability to produce an organisation chart.
5 Ability to interpret an organisation chart.
6 Ability to outline the necessary components of a briefing paper.
7 Production of an information report.
8 Production of a press release.
9 Drafting of a letter of apology.
10 Analysis of a dialogue.

Introduction

Comlon International is a large international conglomerate, whose main activity concerns exploration, extraction, refinement and marketing of oil. The company employs over 2000 people, and is renowned within the energy industry for the relatively small size of its Board of Directors, with five principal, active directors, and a company secretary (see opposite).

The reasons for this are historical. Founded in the UK in 1864, the company made its reputation on the business philosophy of the founder, Mr George Wood, a Glaswegian coal merchant who emerged as one of Scotland's first energy entrepreneurs. Wood built the

* The assistance of the London Chamber of Commerce and Industry, who provided the basis of this case, is gratefully acknowledged.

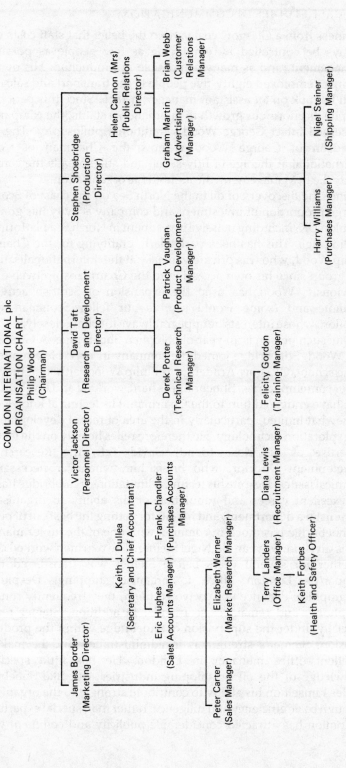

COMLON INTERNATIONAL plc
ORGANISATION CHART

Philip Wood
(Chairman)

James Border
(Marketing Director)

Victor Jackson
(Personnel Director)

David Taft
(Research and Development Director)

Stephen Shoebridge
(Production Director)

Keith J. Dullea
(Secretary and Chief Accountant)

Eric Hughes
(Sales Accounts Manager)

Frank Chandler
(Purchases Accounts Manager)

Peter Carter
(Sales Manager)

Elizabeth Warner
(Market Research Manager)

Terry Landers
(Office Manager)

Diana Lewis
(Recruitment Manager)

Felicity Gordon
(Training Manager)

Keith Forbes
(Health and Safety Officer)

Derek Potter
(Technical Research Manager)

Patrick Vaughan
(Product Development Manager)

Harry Williams
(Purchases Manager)

Helen Cannon (Mrs)
(Public Relations Director)

Graham Martin
(Advertising Manager)

Brian Webb
(Customer Relations Manager)

Nigel Steiner
(Shipping Manager)

business from a Glasgow coal yard in the belief that staff costs would always be controlled by employing as few people as possible in management, and as many as possible in production. His own coal business employed eighty-five people in the transport and sale of coal until he took on an assistant manager in 1876. Since this period, and despite its enormous growth to international status, the company has preserved intact George Wood's traditional philosophy. The great-grandson of George Wood is now the Chairman of Comlon International at the age of fifty-seven and still spreads the company motto 'Lean Management' throughout the organisation.

Since the discovery of oil in the North Sea off the coast of Scotland, a large proportion of investment and company activity has gone into Comlon UK, including massive investment in North Sea platforms and drilling rigs. This has been particularly gratifying for the Chairman, Philip Wood, who was privately uneasy at the 'internationalisation' of the group since his own accession to the Chairmanship twelve years previously. Wood has used the expansion of Scottish activity to promote and (some would say) favour fellow-Scotsman within Comlon, whose interests he appears always to follow closely.

One such person is 49-year-old Stephen Shoebridge. A Glaswegian like Wood, Shoebridge joined the company in 1951. He attended the same school, Glasgow Academy, as Philip Wood, although they were never contemporaries. Shoebridge is hard-working and loyal; qualities that have endeared him to the Chairman. His technical knowledge is somewhat limited, particularly in the area of recent developments in oil exploration technology. He therefore relies heavily on the technical expertise of his close friend, David Taft, the Research and Development Director, who briefs him whenever necessary on technical issues. Despite his technical limitations, Shoebridge has built an excellent career and reputation of his ability to organise and administer a department, and his gift for getting the best out of people.

Shoebridge has much in common with one of the junior managers in his division, 27-year-old Nigel Steiner. The two men worked closely together for several years before Steiner was transferred to the company's London office to organise shipping. Despite the geographical distance now between them, they frequently confer by telephone, and remain close friends. In addition, Steiner remains officially under the supervision of Shoebridge within the production division. Steiner's strength is in administration and he makes an excellent office manager in London. He has little specialised knowledge of the oil or shipping industries, but like Shoebridge, prides himself on his ability to contribute strongly to the organisation through basic efficiency and diligence, rather than special expertise.

Comlon has attracted considerable publicity and comment within the oil industry in the current year because of its development of an oil exploration platform in a sector of the Brae field in the North Sea. The platform is in an area previously thought likely to yield little oil, but the production record of the Comlon platform in its first year has been excellent, so much so that the company has conducted magazine and newspaper advertising around the success of the platform. This success particularly gratifies Philip Wood, who sees it as a Scottish success story and a triumph for Shoebridge's abilities as Production Manager.

Unfortunately, the new drill recently put into service on the Braefield platform in the North Sea has developed a fault. This causes Shoebridge immediate difficulties, as neither he personally nor any of his colleagues have the technical capacity to repair the drill. Taking the advice of David Taft, Shoebridge telexes the Comlon office in Melbourne, Australia, and requests that a specialist consultant and engineer, Jack Foster, should fly urgently to the UK to inspect the installation.

Foster catches the first available Qantas direct flight from Melbourne and is due to arrive in London late one evening. Shoebridge requests that Nigel Steiner should meet Foster and escort him to a specially chartered helicopter for transfer to the platform.

Before leaving Australia, Jack Foster telexes Comlon's Scottish headquarters as follows:

```
4593  13 AUGUST 198X

TO:      STEPHEN SHOEBRIDGE, COMLON, GLASGOW, SCOTLAND, UK

FROM:    JACK FOSTER, COMLON, MELBOURNE, AUSTRALIA


CONFIRM ARRIVE LONDON HEATHROW 2200.  AGREE IMMEDIATE TRANSFER TO
RIG.  PLEASE ENSURE AVAILABILITY AT HEATHROW OF FULL BRIEFING PAPER.
WILL STUDY ON HELICOPTER.
```

The telex arrives in the Glasgow office at 8.30 a.m. and is read by Shoebridge on his arrival. Although it causes him some anxiety, he is unable to consult David Taft about the technical background to the breakdown, as Taft is away at a conference. While he could consult either of Taft's junior managers, he does not do so. Instead, he simply dictates the following briefing report to his secretary.

14 August 198X

RIG ACCIDENT: BRIEFING PAPER

The Comlon North Sea Brae rig has been active since 11 May 1985. The rig
employs a crew of 19, all of whom are on premium pay rates of £90 per day.
The men work a shift of 7 days, interspersed with 2 days' shore leave in
Aberdeen.

A relief crew ensure continual production.

The drill has proved effective and reliable since installation, until malfunction
at 1350 hours on 10 August. At 1445 hours on the same day, the decision was
taken to shut the drill down for fear of causing extensive mechanical damage.
Since this time, crew has been idle but has, of course, remained on station.

The drill was installed during April 1985, at a total cost to Comlon of
£4.6 million.

Our company insurance allows us to recoup repair costs. The principal anxieties
are as follows:

1 High cost of staff, who are experiencing enforced idleness.

2 Loss of revenue from oil barrelage lost (no precise figures available)

3 Loss of status and image - this is a public relations problem, which
   will need the attention of Helen Cannon.

Stephen Shoebridge

S.Shoebridge.

After typing, the briefing report is despatched by courier to Comlon's London office, where it is collected by Nigel Steiner and taken to the airport. Steiner does not read the report.

Foster experiences a delay that which makes his flight from Australia twenty-six hours. On meeting Jack Foster at the airport, Steiner welcomes him and accompanies him to the helicopter pad for departure. While awaiting flight clearance, Steiner gives Foster the briefing report. After a preliminary reading by Foster, and just prior to the helicopter's departure, the following dialogue takes place:

JF: Who the bloody hell wrote this garbage?

NS: The report was produced by our Production Director, Mr Foster. You'll see his signature at the bottom of the report.

JF: Is he a moron or just a time waster?

NS: I don't think he's either. He was my boss for many years and I have a high regard for him.

JF: Yeah, maybe, but this is no good to me. It doesn't tell me anything

I need to know. It's a waste of everyone's time. I'm not interested in what shifts they're doing, I'm here to fix the drill.

NS: We appreciate that Mr Foster and we're very glad to have your expertise. I'm sure the briefing paper will be of some help to you.

JF: No bloody use at all. I'm not surprised you've got yourselves in a tangle if this guy's your Production Director. It's a miracle you're producing anything. This doesn't tell me the position or nature of the breakdown, the maintenance history, the servicing capacity on the rig. I'll need to do all this research myself when I get there. What's wrong, can't your Technical Director write a simple report?

NS: I think I'll find that the Production Department probably is stronger on administration of production than on technical detail, Mr Foster and it's for that reason that you are so invaluable to us. Is there any information that I can get you before you take off, which will be in about five minutes? I can phone or telex from here.

JF: No, no thanks. I'll just make the best of it and get up there sharpish. And, by the way, thanks for meeting me. I'll get on board now.

Foster duly diagnoses and repairs the fault and returns to Australia. However, prior to his departure, Foster sends a letter to Philip Wood pointing out the inadequacy of his briefing and the resultant cost in lost time to the company. The incident concerns Philip Wood, who asks Stephen Shoebridge to write a report, with recommendations, on the entire incident.

Shoebridge feels he cannot do this as he is too closely involved personally, so he delegates the task to Steiner.

Analysis

Answers may be produced by individual work or by small group or class discussion.

1   Examine the organisation chart of Comlon. Did the existing structure of the organisation contribute in any way to the difficulties surrounding the drill breakdown?

2   Consider any factors concerning the traditions and history of the company that may have contributed in some way to the drill crisis. Explain the influence of these factors fully, with precise reference to where and how they were damaging in this case.

3   Identify and explain as fully as possible all of the physical barriers to effective communication in this case.

4   What were the personal and psychological barriers to communication between the following:

(a) Shoebridge and Philip Wood.

(b) Shoebridge and Derek Potter or Patrick Vaughan.
(c) Steiner and Foster.

Planning and solving

- What needs to be accomplished within Comlon in order to prevent a problem of this nature from recurring?
- What needs to be accomplished?
- What needs to be eliminated?
- What needs to be improved?
- What needs to be corrected?

Exercises

1   Identify the weaknesses in

(a) Jack Foster's telex
(b) Stephen Shoebridge's briefing report

Write a full explanation of the communication weaknesses of each document. Explain what a briefing paper should accomplish.

2   You have been asked to recommend changes in the organisation of the company to include the appointment of up to two more managerial staff, if necessary, to eliminate the weaknesses that led to the sequence of events in this case study.

Produce an organisation chart showing what changes you would make. Add explanatory notes that justify your amendments to the existing company structure, and explain how you think your amendments will help internal communication in future.

3   Write a detailed analysis of the dialogue between Steiner and Foster. Consider the following issues:

(a) To what extent was each participant aware of the feelings and position of the other?
(b) Where did real communication take place?
(c) Comment on the tone and style of each participant. Was tone consistent throughout the dialogue, or did it change?
(d) Did either participant influence or control the other at any point?
(e) What were the particular characteristics of the dialogue of each participant?
(f) Did either participant make serious mistakes in the dialogue?
(g) Did either participant show particular skill in dialogue?

4   Draft a letter of apology from Shoebridge to Foster. Bear in mind that it must be an official apology from a senior member of Comlon, not an abject apology. It must not state or imply any weakness in the company or its organisation, but it must repair relations between the two men.

5   As Helen Cannon (Public Relations Director), produce a press release (maximum length, 250 words) on the entire sequence of events, for circulation to national newspapers and energy trade journals, that tries to rescue the prestige image of the Comlon Brae platform, but does not withhold or alter any key facts.

6 · Recruitment at Carefree

This chapter exercises the following skill areas:

1 Design and production of a notice.
2 Design of a checklist for selection interviewing.
3 Design of an application form.
4 Application of suitable tone to the writing of a memo.
5 Researching the resources and facilities of the locality.
6 Recording and presenting findings of research in an oral presentation.
7 Design and production of a pie chart and other notices as appropriate.

Introduction

Carefree Holidays plc is a travel and holiday company with its headquarters in Norway. It has been operating in the UK for only eight years, but has shown spectacular growth in that time, largely due to its ability to offer package holidays to a number of traditionally popular holiday destinations, such as Spain, Majorca and Italy, at very competitive prices.

The company does not sell holidays through high street travel agents, but relies on a heavy and carefully targeted newspaper and TV advertising campaign. The public is then able to telephone bookings direct to Carefree, who in turn control aircraft and hotel reservations by computer. The company's administrative unit is situated at Bromsgrove, Worcestershire, and employs thirty-six people. Thirty of these work in an essentially clerical capacity, with twenty-four telephone sales and confirmation clerks. The job of these clerks is to take telephone bookings, and confirm and log them by using a VDU attached to the company computer. A further five people handle promotional mailing and advertising, under the control of the marketing manager, Mrs Martine Errington. The company's structure at the UK office is illustrated in the diagram opposite.

Knut Bergland, the Managing Director, has been in the UK for only two years. He is twenty-nine years old and firmly committed to the idea of achieving profitability through cost containment and managerial efficiency. He realises that he must show further success

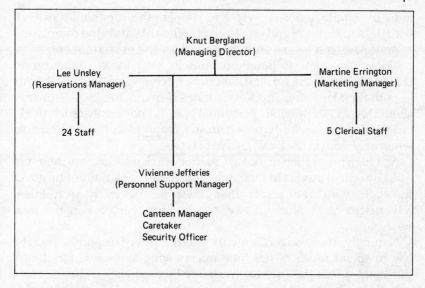

in the UK operation to develop his own career with the company. Ideally, he would hope to be transferred to the United States after three successful years running the UK operation at Bromsgrove.

Lee Unsley is thirty-two years old, an enthusiastic student of computer systems. His background is as computer manager with a nationwide car rental company, and he is rather absorbed in the technical issues of running a computerised Reservations department. Bergland does not mind the fact that he is rather isolated, as he obtains excellent results and operates an efficient division.

Martine Errington is thirty-three years old and has always worked in the area of sales and marketing. She is highly aggressive and ambitious, but relates very well to those around her and loves to discuss and resolve work-based problems by holding group discussions with Bergland and anyone else who will join in. She is highly sociable, and believes that any company issues should be discussed and resolved by everyone.

The staff is completed by the Personnel Support Manager, who is also responsible for the day-to-day operations of the building, and she controls the three support staff of the Canteen Manager, Caretaker and Security Officer.

The post of Personnel and Support Manager is held by Vivienne Jefferies, a 52-year-old widow who joined Carefree two years previously, following redundancy, after spending twenty-one years as a personnel officer with a large Midlands motor manufacturer. Although she is unused to working in small organisations, and is uneasy about her own lack of familiarity with a computerised service industry employing relatively few people, she communicates well with the support staff and is reasonably efficient within the company.

Knut Bergland has recently given her control of recruitment, as he no longer has time to handle it himself. Vivienne is, therefore, in charge of advertising for staff, selection interviewing for clerical posts in both the Marketing and Reservations Departments. She is uneasy about this, as her previous personnel post did not involve such work, but she does not seek advice or help and simply places advertisements when necessary in the local newspaper.

As a high proportion of jobs at Carefree are clerical, and are therefore filled by school leavers in their first post, there is a significant turnover in staff, with the result that Vivienne places a recruitment advertisement as often as twenty-two times per year in the local newspaper.

Naturally, these advertisements attract a heavy response, and she has to spend much of her time interviewing applicants for clerical positions, a task she tries to streamline by producing a checklist (see pages 43 and 44), and keeping her interviews to a maximum of twenty minutes.

Knut Bergland is uneasy about the recruitment processes of the company. Both Martine Errington and Lee Unsley have complained that they receive a high proportion of employees who are unsuitably immature, with no conception of what their job involves. Bergland is suspicious that the interviewing process is not sufficiently thorough and does little to assess the qualities of patience and ability to adapt to regular routine that are needed in clerical posts. He decides to review the selection processes that Vivienne Jefferies manages and sends her a memo (see page 45).

She has never given an oral report to a group of managers before, always having written her reports. She senses that the other managers would like someone younger in her job, and realises she must give a positive, decisive and brief report that will propose solutions to the problems that she realises exist.

She lists the following points which she wants to convey:

1   Sum spent on advertising for staff, 198X – £1750.
    Sum spent on candidates' travel expenses – £625.
    Sum spent on letters to local schools, chamber of commerce, etc. information of vacancies – £100.00.
2   Strengths and weaknesses of current system.
3   Possible alternative methods of recruitment; cost of each method.

She feels that if she can support her presentation with a number of charts and visual aids, she will be convincing. She also plans to

Carefree Holidays plc

APPLICATION FOR EMPLOYMENT

FORENAMES   SURNAME

ADDRESS   TEL.NO.

JOB APPLIED FOR

REASONS FOR WANTING JOB

PREVIOUS JOBS

SCHOOLS ATTENDED SINCE AGE 11, WITH EXAM RESULTS

NAMES AND ADDRESSES OF TWO REFEREES

---

conclude her presentation with some definite proposals for future recruitment. She decides the presentation must take no more than ten minutes in all.

Carefree Holidays plc

INTERVIEW CHECKLIST

1 Appearance

2 Punctuality

3 School Results

4 Hobbies

5 Religion

6 Career Plans

7 Verbal Fluency

8 Manners

9 Headmaster's Reference

Analysis

1 Assess the strengths and weaknesses of Vivienne's press advertisement.

2 What personal and psychological factors make Vivienne's position at the company difficult?

3 What was wrong with Bergland's memo? What unnecessary/unfortunate effects did it have?

4 What are the communication problems within the company? Identify these and rank them in order of importance.

5 What are the communication problems between the company itself and the outside community?

Carefree Holidays plc

MEMO

To   Vivienne Jefferies

From Knut Bergland

Date 24 July 198X

RECRUITMENT

Recruitment is costing us too much here. We must
make savings of 50 per cent on our budget at once.
Less press advertising, more cost-free promotion.
Please research these and report to myself, Lee and
Martine a week today.

Are our interviews efficient enough? Please show
me the checklist you use to evaluate people coming
here for interviews and the application form you
use.

Why is our press advertising getting poor results
by attracting too few people and not enough good
candidates?

Please cover all this in your (oral) report.

KB

Planning and solving

Having considered the case, consider each of the following:

- What is to be accomplished overall?
- What is to be corrected?
- What is to be improved?
- What is to be eliminated?

List these considerations and rank them in order of importance.

Pick any two of these considerations and outline two possible solutions for each. Briefly note the advantages and drawbacks of each solution.

Exercises

The exercises that follow may be taken singly or as an integrated group.

1   Design a notice to be circulated to all free outlets (such as public library, careers office, etc.) in which you encourage school leavers to approach Carefree for employment. The notice should be eye-catching and informative, but should be careful not to raise false hopes.

2   Design a checklist that would improve on Vivienne's checklist and be more useful for interviewing for clerical positions at Carefree.

3   Design an application form that would be more informative and up to date than Vivienne's, and that would provide a better basis for an initial interview of a school leaver.

4   Prepare notes and visual aids as necessary to conduct Vivienne's presentation to the rest of the management team.

5   Imagine that your own town is the centre of Carefree's operation. By doing research in the locality, compile a report on free sources of publicity and referral for the company to use when seeking employees. Consider, among others, the following:

The Job Centre
The Careers Service of the local education authority
The local public libraries
The Borough Information Office
Local radio
The Manpower Services Commission

6   Imagine that you are Vivienne. Produce any notes and visual aids (including a pie chart on current recruitment costs) for use at your oral presentation.

7   Imagine that you are Vivienne, and make an eight-minute oral presentation to the management team. The remainder of your class will assess you using the criteria on the oral presentation checklist at the end of Chapter 3.

8   Re-write Bergland's memo in a more appropriate tone.

7 · Tartan Fashions Ltd*

This case study is designed to exercise the following skill areas:

1 Appreciation of issues of non-verbal communication in a commercial context.
2 Appreciation of the relationship between physical layout of the work place and working efficiency.
3 Appreciation of the relationship between the physical layout of the workplace and working relationships.
4 An understanding of the importance of questionnaires in market research.
5 Ability to conduct research on point of sale marketing.
6 Design of a training programme.
7 Appreciation of the value of computerisation to stock control and to delivery.

Introduction

Tartan Fashions Ltd was established in Scotland in the early 1900s and manufactured jewellery for the women's fashion market in Scotland. As the company grew, it relocated to Birmingham, so that it could easily reach all parts of the UK for retailing operations. The company's success to date has been characterised by rapid expansion brought about by an alert senior management team. The policy of the company is to be continually aware of market gaps and the possibility of introducing new products.

Up until 1983, the company had favoured an austere, conventional and expensive product range, which, although characterised by new products, was aimed solely at the established, and rather limited market of the 30 to 55-year-old woman, with conventional taste and significant disposable income. In order to reach this market, the company has adopted the strategy of renting 'store within a store' units in the larger and more prestigious fashion and department stores in all of Britain's major cities. Examples include Selfridges and Liberty's in London, Rackham's in Birmingham and Bainbridge's in Newcastle.

* With acknowledgements to the Institute of Marketing.

Currently, the company is running fourteen such units, which are successful within the rather staid and limited market in which they operate.

However, the directors feel that these units have become too established, and that a programme of re-training of staff and overall re-organisation could achieve very much better results, when coupled to the new expansions in the product range planned for late 1986.

The Sales Director, Simon Whitehead, is therefore delegated to produce a performance study on each of the units, commenting on strengths and weaknesses in current operations, and suggesting amendments in the image, house style, operations and product range of the company that would yield better results, and would enable the company to expand into the market for the 15–25 age group, without losing support in its conventional and established markets.

Whitehead's background includes eight years as a regional sales manager, supervising the West Midlands region, and covering four 'store within a store' units, and another sixteen high street jewellers. He is thus very confident of his ability to monitor the existing operation. However, his understanding and experience in the young fashion jewellery market is minimal and so he plans to rely heavily on the feedback he gains from retailing staff, who are in daily contact with customers, and who have a strong sense of the local competition.

Each 'store within a store' is controlled by Whitehead's own office, which supplies them with the full product range and with accompanying point of sale publicity. Tartan Fashions uses house colours of olive green and mustard yellow, which form the tartan attire worn by all sales staff, and the company logo, an olive thistle mounted against a velvet fabric in mustard yellow. The effect of discreet and established comfort and luxury has characterised the Tartan house style since the early 1950s.

The jewellery trade is one in which instant purchase accounts for a high proportion of trade. Few customers place orders for particular items and then wait for delivery; sales are much more likely to be achieved by good customer reception and management, excellent layout, and efficient stock control in order to maximise the unit's ability to produce the necessary lines on demand by the customer.

No media advertising is conducted, except for an annual advertisement in magazines such as *Women's Journal* and *The Lady* that consists of photographs of the year's new lines.

However, the company puts significant resources into point of sale promotion, providing expensive tent cards for counter-top display, direction signs to lead to the Tartan unit within a store, and double crown posters and shelf stickers to attract attention further.

Whitehead is very satisfied with this arrangement for retaining the traditional markets of the company, but he feels strongly that the newly diversified product range will need different promotional instruments. This is another reason behind his tour of branches. The need to compare existing practices with anticipated needs is another reason for his tour of branches.

He begins his tour in the south-west region, visiting the store in Bristol initially. The Tartan unit is located on the ground floor of the department store. The layout of the ground floor is as shown:

Layout of ground floor, XXX store, Bristol

The 'store within a store' concept (see page 50) means that good stock control is of particular importance, as storage space is very limited (400 cu.ft. per unit). The company also likes to keep the bulk of its stock in the far more secure warehouse that the company has at its Birmingham headquarters. The company has an agreement with its insurers that no more than £85 000 worth of stock is to be held at any one branch.

Therefore, each unit telephones headquarters fortnightly, in order to briefly report on stock shortages, and to submit an order. Whitehead is considering employing a clerk to handle submitted forms from all

Layout of Tartan's 'store within a store' unit

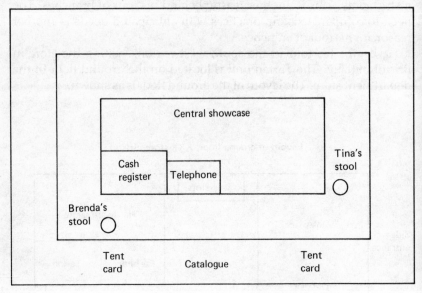

the branches, in view of the high number of errors involved in telephone stock control.

On his arrival, Whitehead finds that the Tartan unit is permanently staffed by two operatives: Brenda Mullin, who is unit supervisor, aged forty-seven, and who has worked in retail sales in Bristol throughout her working life. She is extremely happy to have a job at Bristol's premier store, and considers herself lucky to be dealing with relatively wealthy people who have money to spend, and who appreciate good service. She also enjoys the responsibility of supervising the unit. She takes little interest in the jewellery industry at large, although she is proud of her knowledge of the Tartan catalogue, believing that she knows the price and description of every item by heart. She is a firm believer in the idea of discreetly efficient selling and is never overtly 'pushy' in her treatment of customers. She regards her uniform with some pride, and is very content to wear it and to promote Tartan products at every opportunity.

Tina Pope is seventeen, and has joined Tartan in Bristol on the Youth Training Scheme. She is glad to be working in the fashion industry, but would like to have an opportunity to sell to people of her own age, which does not present itself at Tartan. She believes personality to be more important than uniform, and is sceptical of acquired sales techniques. When Whitehead arrives to spend the morning with them, he is conscious of a certain gulf between them, although they are courteous to each other. When Pope arrives, he notices the layout of the unit, and asks Brenda to explain the reasons for the layout she has chosen. Brenda explains as follows:

'I chose to be near hardware because the contrast is fantastic; it makes our jewellery look so luxurious. Also, I like the idea of a central showcase, so psychologically it makes the products seem a bit more special and exalted, more so than they would be if we only had glass counters between us and the customer. You'll also notice that we have a compact customer service unit, with catalogue and cash register and 'phone for credit card authorisation very close together. This means that there's speed and efficiency in processing customers, and about 80 per cent of space where they can browse casually – always a good thing in this business. Tina's taking the other side for security reasons, and she can see the life of the street, which is nice when she's not busy. You'll see that the tent cards flank the catalogue, and focus on it nicely.'

Following this discussion, Whitehead invites Brenda to take her coffee break and talks with Tina. He learns that she feels disappointed that the job is not enabling her to sell to people of her own age, and she welcomes the news of Tartan's plans for product development. However, she does not supply Whitehead with any ideas about possible trends in costume jewellery and the conversation soon peters out. Whitehead walks round the store. He returns to find Tina sitting on her stool, smoking and reading a newspaper. She is quite absorbed, and does not notice the middle-aged customer standing by the cash register. Her attention is finally drawn when the customer raps the counter continually with a coin. The following conversation takes place:

TINA: Oh, yes please?

CLIENT: Ah, I would like to see some strings of plain pearls, with a gold clasp mechanism, please.

TINA: Yes, they're all in the main case in front of you. That is except for our top range; they're £1200 and they're kept in the central showcase. Security, you see. But I can't show them until my supervisor gets back from coffee with the key.

CLIENT: Are they cultured?

TINA: Er? Er, I don't know. Can you look in the catalogue; it's just by those big cards.

CLIENT: Your range does seem rather limited; do you only have what's in the showcase?

TINA: Oh no. We don't carry the company's entire range here. You can order from the catalogue, but there's two to three weeks delivery, unless it's on tomorrow's van; they only deliver fortnightly, and even the regional depot might not have it. But I'll try if you like . . .

CLIENT: Does it speed matters if I pay by credit card? You could get a 'phone authorisation and I would be happy to pay extra for courier delivery if it would expedite matters.

TINA: Oh, can you wait for Miss Mullin? She handles all these special orders . . .

Analysis

1   Discuss the extent to which the Bristol operation does and does not match up to the established house style of Tartan.
2   Identify the strengths of Miss Mullin's layout of the stall.
3   What evidence does the case study offer of the need for training of Brenda?
4   To what extent can the shortcomings of the Bristol operation be attributed to failures of internal communication within Tartan?

Planning and solving

- What needs to be accomplished?
- What needs to be eliminated?
- What needs to be improved?
- What needs to be introduced?

List the problems that have entirely local causes in this case. Which problems are the responsibility of regional management, outside the store?

Exercises

1   Write a detailed analysis of the customer's exchange with Tina, identifying the communications strengths and breakdowns of each speaker, and any implications for sales training.
2   Examine the layout of the Tartan unit. What objections can be raised to the organisation of the unit?
3   On the basis of what you identify in the shortcomings of Brenda Mullin's performance as supervisor, design a one-day training course in supervisory management for all Tartan 'store within a store' supervisors.
4   Design a questionnaire (see Glossary) for use by Simon Whitehead with all retail staff. The purposes of the questionnaire are to monitor the following issues:

   (a) Profile of current customers (age, income, tastes, etc.).
   (b) Customer attitudes to Tartan's image and house style.
   (c) Customer perceptions of shortcomings in the Tartan product range.

(d) Customer attitudes to levels of service they receive from Tartan.

5   Conduct a study (based on your local shops) in which you compare point of sale advertising of jewellery with point of sale advertising of hi-fi equipment. Identify and explain the differences in approach and presentation of advertising.

6   Explain how computerisation could assist the efficiency of stock control and delivery within this organisation.

8 · Minitron Ltd*

This chapter exercises the following skills:

1 Appreciation of the importance of stock control.
2 Design of a stock control form.
3 Appreciation of the application of computers to stock control.
4 Appreciation of the relationship between organisational structure and the quality of communication.
5 Production of a recommendation report.
6 Summary of a source document.
7 Production of an organisation chart.
8 Production of a research study comparing costs of an essential service.
9 Production of a press release.
10 Production of a recruitment advertisement.

Introduction

Minitron Ltd is a small company that designs and manufactures complex electronic machinery, such as instruments for the motor and aerospace industries and consumer electronic goods. The company was founded seven years ago by Vaughan Wingdale, an American who had settled in the UK after spending many years studying at Cambridge University, followed by some years in the aerospace industry. The company now produces a range of eight machines. However, the biggest sellers are a calculator and a personal computer, and these two items account for 80 per cent of output.

Some components have to be imported from the USA and Japan, and thus need to be ordered eight weeks in advance of their likely use in assembly, compared with three weeks for UK suppliers and five weeks for EEC countries (a West German plastics firm supplies the casings used in Minitron's personal computers).

Wingdale himself remains interested in the development side of the business rather than in production or marketing. As the company grows, he finds that he quickly needs to appoint two senior managers,

* With acknowledgements to the Institute of Administrative Management and to the Industrial Society.

one for production and the other for purchasing and supply.
Marketing is handled by an external marketing and public relations
firm, Webcom International, who place advertisements and negotiate
with the company's wholesale clients.

Both senior managers are appointed from the computer and
electronics industry; Diana Weekes is controller for purchasing and
supply and has previously worked in an audio and hi-fi company, and
Carl Wright, who is an American production manager with experience
in the Californian electronics industry and an old acquaintance of
Wingdale.

Minitron has experienced exceptionally fast growth and now has
factories in Liverpool, south-west London and Southampton, with
each factory producing the full range of machines and each operating
under a General Manager. The three General Managers report to the
senior management team of Wingdale, Wright and Diana Weekes,
who are based at Southampton.

Carl Wright notices from monthly statistics that the south-west
London factory has a better production record than the other two
plants. This intrigues him as manning and equipment is at identical
levels in each plant. He eventually traces the discrepancy to its cause:
the London plant receives overseas delivery more promptly than any
of the others. In particular, two key components, capacitors from
Japan and computer casings from West Germany, are frequently
stockpiled at the London plant, while production at the others is
running more slowly. He realises that he needs to find a method of
monitoring stock levels at each of these key components at each plant
on a daily basis. After consulting with the General Manager of each
plant, he agrees that the Personal Assistant to each General Manager
will send a daily telex to each of the other General Managers,
informing on stock levels. Each plant will also keep a tally of weekly
production needs, so that stock level needs may be predicted with
some accuracy. Copies of all telexes will be sent to Wright himself at
his office adjoining the Southampton site.

Wright plans to monitor stock levels and to submit orders to Diana
Weekes for placement with suppliers in the UK, Japan and West
Germany.

Diana plans to use either a road freight service or British Rail to move
stock from one plant to another. As a carton of 500 capacitors weighs
only 4 kg and is 80 cm × 40 cm × 40 cm, transportation should not be
too costly. In the case of the computer casing, however, each case is
individually packaged, weighs 3.5 kg and has dimensions of 35 cm ×
20 cm × 10 cm.

Diana anticipates having to freight as many as 700 cases and 1500
individual capacitors per week to 'juggle' stocks around the
company's plants.

Various rumours have been spreading on the company grapevine. One was that the Liverpool factory was to close and production move to London where they expect to need more employees. Another was that production of the best-selling machine was to be switched to a company at Besançon in France, whose brand-new highly automated production facilities had been subsidised by the French Government. A Member of Parliament for Liverpool has tabled a question of the House of Commons about this, and representatives of the media are asking for interviews.

Union officials in Liverpool have threatened to call a protest strike, and are demanding to see their General Manager, who rang the Managing Director at headquarters this morning to ask how to proceed.

Wingdale himself realises that he is not a good communicator, and that the staff at the three factories need to be brought into closer contact with senior management. However, he has neither the time nor the money to develop this, so he asks Paul Webster, Managing Director of Webcom International, to brief him on inexpensive methods of internal communication, such as notice boards and a monthly company bulletin for all employees.

Wingdale is also acutely nervous about handling relations with the media, and does not want to talk to them direct.

A final problem is that, following the rumour (which is unfounded) about the likely closure of the Liverpool plant, the company has found it difficult to recruit night shift workers, with the result that the night shift is now 20 per cent undermanned, with a 20 per cent production shortfall . . .

Analysis

1 Identify and list each problem of internal communication faced by the company.

2 Identify and list each problem of external communication faced by the company.

3 To what extent can the problems of the company be attributed to its management organisation and structure? (*Note*: do not consider geographial diversions in this question.)

Planning and solving

- What needs to be eliminated?
- What needs to be accomplished?
- What needs to be improved?
- What needs to be corrected?

Using and placing posters and notice boards

Posters and notice boards are used by a large number of firms. The localities for the boards are generally at central positions, at canteens, near clocking-in and checking-out points and so on.

The disadvantages of using clocking-in and checking-out points is that employees are often in a hurry and will not linger to look at notice boards.

A survey on Joint Consultation by the National Institute of Industrial Psychology found:

> So little thought was given to the position of notice boards by many firms that they placed them by the time clocks; this virtually ensured that notices posted on them would not be read, for there tends to be a crowd round the time clocks in the morning, while at closing time people rush past them. One firm with two geographically separated sections had the minutes posted by the time clocks in one section and in a central position in the other. It was found that there was considerably more interest shown in the section where they were centrally posted. A significant association was found between the interest of the workers and the practice of posting minutes on the notice boards.
>
> Providing that the material is changed frequently, and that it is attractive and readable, employees will get into the habit of looking at the notice boards. The boards should also be protected from the weather, well lighted and secure from tampering; the messages on them should be brief and timely.
>
> The poster technique has proved its usefulness for advertising purposes, and there is no reason to suppose that, handled efficiently, it should not also make a useful contribution to industrial communication.

Suggestion schemes and safety are two frequent subjects for use in posters. In the Esso Petroleum Company these types of posters are designed by employees. Competitions are held in order to obtain the best ideas for designs. Although the posters are drawn by professional artists, they carry the name of the employees who designed them. The advantage of this scheme is that the competition creates a good deal of interest in the subject, and the fact that the posters carry such inscriptions as 'Designed by Driver Joe Smith' certainly helps to dispel any impression that the publicity is coming from an impersonal source in Head Office. (Taken from Cecil Chisholm, 'Communication in Industry', Industrial Society)

Exercises

1   Design a stock control form for daily use by the Personal Assistant to the General Manager in each factory. The form is to cover the weekly needs of each plant for the two key components, existing stock levels and an indication of whether shipments will either be needed from other plants, or will be possible to make to other plants.

2   Write a brief outline (250 words maximum) explaining how computerisation could help both stock control and purchasing at Minitron.

3   Draw an organisation chart of the company.

4   Identify the key 'pressure points' on this chart where communication is poor.

5   Produce an organisation chart that shows how, with existing staffing and sites, the internal communication problems of the company could be reduced by re-organisation.

6   Research a comparative study on the costs and relative benefits of despatching stocks by road, rail or by the Post Office.

7   Write a recommendation report (see Glossary) as Paul Webster to Vaughan Wingdale on the potential value and possible pitfalls of notice boards and monthly bulletins (maximum 400 words).

You may use the extract from *Communication in Industry* as a basis for your report.

8   Write a press release for Vaughan Wingdale that refutes the rumour of the Liverpool closure.

9   Design an advertisement (60 words maximum) to go into the local newspaper, with the aim of recruiting night shift workers for unskilled assembly.

9 · The Gondola chain*

This case study is designed to exercise understanding in the following areas:

1 The importance of a job description for interviewer and interviewee.
2 The use of personnel specifications for interviewers.
3 The importance of a curriculum vitae for interviewer and interviewee.
4 The relationship between a curriculum vitae and the content and course of a selection interview.
5 The principal types of question employed in a selection interview, including open, closed, probe, reflective and check questions.
6 Skills in preparing for an interview on the part of both interviewer and interviewee.

Introduction

The Doolish Group is a large conglomerate with many interests, including Snaesnax, a fast food company whose product range is designed to support a chain of restaurants that will provide competition to existing fast food chains, but with the aim of becoming known as the market leader in fast food, with quality service, and a sufficiently broad appeal to attract shoppers and businessmen for lunch, and families in the evening. It is decided to call the chain 'Gondola' restaurants, because of the association with comfort, wealth and the unusual. Because of these very ambitious plans, Snaesnax are placing emphasis on recruitment of suitable staff. Each restaurant will have an overall manager, responsible for operations in both the kitchen and the 'front of house' area, where there will be a need to control waitresses, cashiers and security staff.

Rosanne Beamish is the Senior Personnel Executive for Snaesnax, and is currently spending all her time drafting employment contracts for the staff who will be appointed to the new restaurants. She, therefore, has little time to co-ordinate a recruitment programme to

* My thanks are due to the Royal Society of Arts and to the Industrial Society for material used in this case study.

generate the new staff who will be needed when the twenty-seven new Snaesnax restaurants have their nationally co-ordinated launch in April.

The situation is particularly difficult in the north-east where the company has taken leases in prime locations in Stockton, Darlington and Middlesbrough, but has no staff and no experience in those areas, as neither Snaesnax nor any of the other companies in the Doolish Group have interests there.

It is therefore decided that Rosanne's deputy, Andrew Tatham, will travel from the Head Office of Snaesnax in Manchester to spend approximately ten days based in a hotel in Middlesbrough. He will devote this time entirely to staff recruitment.

It is decided to recruit three restaurant managers through local advertising, with appointment to begin six weeks prior to the opening date. This interval period is to be used by the restaurant managers to prepare for the opening, including the appointment of chef, cashier, security and waitressing staff.

Judith Samuelson has a strong background in catering, having worked for many years as the reservations and table manageress for the dining room of the largest hotel in Stockton-on-Tees. This experience, coupled with excellent references, is enough to gain her appointment as manageress of the Middlesbrough 'Gondola', despite her lack of experience in appointing staff, or in managing anyone other than waitresses. However, as pressure of time is great, her first task is to place advertisements and to recruit kitchen, security and cashier staff. She receives little help from Tatham, as he has to supervise a number of other managerial appointments at other branches.

As the restaurant is still being decorated, Judith decides to conduct interviews in the conference room of a hotel in Darlington, which she rents for three days.

Following a campaign of advertising both in the local Job Centre and in the local press, she makes appointments to interview nine people for the post of restaurant security officer on the morning of 10 February.

The first candidate is Keith Clayton, who has sent a letter of application (see opposite) and his curriculum vitae (see page 62).

JS: Ah, do come in, Mr Clayton. I'm glad you were able to be punctual, especially as we have to make an early start. Was your journey easy?
KC: Yes, thanks.
JS: How did you get here, by the way?
KC: My father works just along the way at the Council, so he gave me a lift.

12 Kirby Heights
Darlington

2 February 1986

Dear Manageress

I am writing in answer to your advertisement for a security officer in the Job Centre, Darlington. I enclose details of myself. I hope to hear from you.

Yours sincerely

K D Clayton

JS: Yes, very useful. Now, can you tell me why you would like to be a security officer?

KC: Well . . . er . . . it's steady work, isn't it? And I quite like the idea of mixing with people . . . working with people.

JS: Have you worked with people much in your career up to now?

KC: Well, no, not really. You see, I used to be a clerk, in quite a small office. We didn't meet many people there, really, only the three of us. But when I was with the theatre company I met more people, and that I quite did like. I certainly preferred it to working in an office.

JS: What made you go to the theatre company? It must have been an interesting move from your first job.

KC: Well, two chaps I'd been friendly with from school wanted to try this travelling theatre. They knew I could paint scenery from school,

```
K. D. CLAYTON

PERSONAL AND WORK HISTORY


Date of birth:      11 January 1961

Place of birth:     Darlington

Secondary school:   Darlington County Secondary School

Date left school:   June 1976


Exams passed:       O level Art
                    CSE Grade 3 Geography
                    CSE Grade 3 English
                    CSE Grade 4 Mathematics
                    CSE Grade 2 Metalwork

Hobbies at school: Football, scenery design for drama


Employment:  Sept 1976-Feb 1978 - Clerk, Housing Office,
                                   Darlington District Council

             Feb 1978-Aug 1978  - Vanguard Travelling Theatre,
                                   Stage Manager

             Jan 1981-Sept 198X - Clerk, Rowson Transport Ltd,
                                   Darlington


I am unmarried and live with my parents.  My hobbies are
television, painting and football.
```

so they asked me to join. It was interesting but then winter came on and we couldn't travel to seaside places, it got a bit of a drag, and we weren't making the money. So I went to Rowsons.

JS: Yes . . . you met a lot of people in the Vanguard Theatre?

KC: Yes, that's right. Lots of them. More than at Rowsons or the Council.

JS: Yes, I see . . . Well, what do you think being a security officer for a new restaurant would involve?

KC: I don't know really. Perhaps you could tell me a few details?

JS: Yes, of course. Well, it's the usual security duties, you know. Watching the cash, looking out for trouble, that sort of thing. How do you think it would be different in a restaurant from anywhere else?

KC: Well, the hours, I suppose. Start late, finish late, I should think.

And I suppose you'd have to be very careful about drunks. I mean, when to turn a blind eye and when to ask them to leave, that sort of thing.

JS: Yes, that's a good point.

KC: I mean, perhaps I can turn the question back on you a bit. What does the job really involve?

JS: Well, it's pretty much as you've described it really. We would want the officer to take money to the bank, I suppose.

KC: What about keeping an eye on the other staff, watching for stock pilferage, that sort of thing? That was a big problem at Rowsons.

JS: Well, possibly, but at this stage I couldn't really be all that specific. Er, could you tell me something about your schooldays?

KC: Well, it's rather a long time ago now. What was it you wanted to know?

JS: Oh, your interests and activities, that sort of thing.

KC: Yes, as I said on the letter, I liked football. I was always in the school team, and then painting the scenery for drama. That was about it.

JS: Could you tell me which CSEs and O levels you got again?

KC: Yes, O level Art and CSEs in English, Maths, Geography and Metalwork.

JS: I wonder how far the examination system in schools really helps people to prepare for their working life . . .

KC: I wonder.

JS: Yes, fine . . . what do you think would be your major difficulty as a security officer?

KC: I suppose it might get rather boring. Monotonous, you know, standing around and just waiting for trouble. If there weren't opportunities for change and for promotion, it would soon get a bit dull, I reckon. But I would like it. I would like to work with people, relaxed, in a place like a restaurant.

JS: Would you describe yourself as a relaxed sort of person?

KC: I suppose so.

JS: Have you applied for any other jobs as a security officer?

KC: No, this is the first one. I think it was the idea of working in the centre of town, working with people in a busy restaurant, that attracted me. And your advert, of course. That was very eye-catching.

JS: Yes, of course. Now, I do have to ask you if you have any disabilities, any history of serious illnesses, or any criminal convictions.

KC: No, nothing like that. One speeding fine on my motor bike four years ago, but that wasn't a criminal offence, of course.

JS: And do you have any other job applications in at the moment?

KC: Not at the moment, no.

JS: Well, thank you very much for coming in. Do you have any questions for me?

KC: No, thank you.

JS: I hope I'll be able to write to you later this week. Would you take the job if we offered it to you?

KC: Oh yes. Yes, I'd take it.

JS: Well, thank you again for coming. I hope we'll meet again. Goodbye.

Analysis

What problems were faced by Judith Samuelson before she began interviewing?

Which of these problems originated from Snaesnax's central organisation and decisions?

Which of the problems had local origin and could have been avoided had Judith anticipated and planned more effectively?

How far was the difficulty of the interviewing exercise caused by a failure in communication between Snaesnax's Head Office personnel (Rosanne Beamish and Andrew Tatham) and Judith?

Planning and solving

From the point of view of Snaesnax Ltd explain:

- What needs to be accomplished?
- What needs to be eliminated?
- What needs to be improved?
- What needs to be introduced?

Exercises

1 Read the extract on 'preparing for an interview' from the Industrial Society book on interviewing skills. Write a critique on the strengths and weaknesses of Judith's preparation.

2 Comment on the range and mix of Judith's questions (see Appendix 2).

3 In what way would a detailed job description have affected the interview?

4 Complete a job description for the vacancy.

5 Study the example of a personnel specification enclosed. What would this interview have gained if Judith had had a personnel specification while conducting the interview? Complete a personnel specification for the vacancy.

6 Identify all the shortcomings of Keith Clayton's letter of application and curriculum vitae. Re-write the curriculum vitae in such a way that it presents a stronger case for his suitability for the vacancy.

7   Comment on the quality of Keith's preparation for the interview, in the light of the extract on preparing for an interview.

8   Summarise both the extracts, and write a checklist for candidates who are attending selection interviews on 'Points to bear in mind when preparing for an interview'.

Preparing to conduct an interview

Preparation

Preparation is crucial. Much of the success of a selection interview depends on thorough preparation. This need not take hours, just good planning. For instance, six interviews for one job does not entail going through all the preparatory steps six times – only the application forms and interview plans need studying before each one.

It is important to be clear about what the job involves and what sort of person could fulfil it. From a comparison of the application form with this information an interview plan can be sketched out to expand and supplement the information on it. This should be a list of areas needing to be covered rather than an inflexible timetable. It is important as a checklist during the interview – it is surprising how often the simpler questions slip the mind during the anxiety of the occasion. 'I don't need a plan – I know all about this job and I know what I'm looking for' sounds marvellous before the interview, but often leaves the interviewer desperately searching for something to say during the interview itself – very few people are spontaneously good – it would be rather arrogant and foolhardy for most of us to rely on spontaneous genius emerging. We need therefore to prepare the following:

- Job description (a written picture of the job to be filled) (see page 66).
- Person specification (a written picture of the person needed to do the job) (see page 67).
- Application form (how does it compare with the example on page 43?)
- Interview plan (headings of areas needing discussion or answers).
- Assessment system (some way of assessing one candidate against another).
- Company information (company structure, other locations, products, pensions, sick pay, social club, loans and conditions of services, etc.).
- Environment (will the candidate be greeted at reception, is the room layout suitable, is tea/coffee arranged, can interruptions be minimised or stopped, etc?).
- Relevant legislation – do I know about it?

Personnel specification

Senior personnel records clerk

1	Physical	Age 25–40.
2	Attainments	Good clerical experience, preferably in personnel records work or involving filing/elementary figure-work.
3	Intelligence	Needs to be quick enough to learn personnel system and organisation of company in terms of persons to liaise with. Use of initiative in organising and handling work.
4	Aptitudes	Typing, clear handwriting, able to communicate with other people, including senior people in organisation. Numerical facility – simple statistics and calculations.
5	Interests	Needs to be someone who will get on with other people – social interests could be a pointer.
6	Disposition	Able to work under pressure at times. Must be trustworthy for confidential information.
7	Circumstances	Must be able to travel to work easily. Regular attendance essential – family ties or commitments must not conflict with job.

Person specification

Job . . . . Department . . . .

	Desirable	Essential
		State requirements in columns

1 Physical requirements,
   e.g. stamina, appearance,
   health, speech

2 Attainments
   (a)Level of education
      special skills/
      occupational training
   (b)Experience or other
      requirement

3 General intelligence

4 Special aptitudes,
   e.g. spatial perception,
   good writing ability

5 Interests
   Do they indicate anything
   about the person?
   Do they conflict?

6 Disposition: Stability
                 Acceptability
                 Self-reliance
                 Leadership

7 Domestic circumstances

Signed . . . . Date . . . .

Skills

- Ask open questions to get the conversation going and to encourage the interviewee to talk.
- Make sure that all facts are drawn out by using specific questions.
- Start with an easy leading question if the candidate is shy or retiring.
- Have any hypothetical questions ready prepared before the interview starts. These are invaluable in the selection interview to test how the individual would think through and approach a problem. It also tests the person's knowledge. Ask these sort of questions when the interviewee has 'settled in' – later rather than sooner – they can be nerve racking.

Probe. Never accept a partial answer or one that dodges the question – probe the answer for more details. If you are suspicious of an answer, probe by asking it again in a different guise – you may find out more. (The text of this section is taken from J. Grummit, 'Interviewing Skills', the Industrial Society.)

10 · Beaumanor Golf Club (1)*

This chapter is designed to exercise the following skills:

1 Using tact and manipulating tone in writing a letter of warning.
2 Writing a letter of explanation.
3 Producing a circular.
4 Producing a briefing paper.
5 Producing a poster.
6 Appreciating the benefits of a microcomputer system within an organisation.
7 Expressing these benefits in report form, clearly understandable to a layman.
8 Appreciating the relationship between organisational structure and the quality of internal communication.
9 Appreciation of the psychological and institutional factors underlying communication problems.
10 Design and producing of a questionnaire.

Introduction

Beaumanor is a pleasant and affluent suburb of the fringes of Shrewsbury, a medium-sized town in the central west of England, with a population of 200 000. The town is a centre for agriculture, and for a variety of light industries, many of which have been attracted to the region in the past twenty years by the steadily increasing quality of road transport links to the Birmingham conurbation, and thence to the rest of the UK and its ports.

The club was founded in the early 1960s, initially by a group of retired businessmen, who bought the old manor house and grounds on the edge of Beaumanor, and established a nine-hole golf course there. The membership remained small, and the club select, until the late 1970s, when many of the founding generation had died, or given up golf. The club's membership has, therefore, been in decline for the past ten years. In 198X, the club's management committee decided that the club needed to alter its strategy in order to survive. It appointed Bernard Jones as manager. Bernard was a young

* With acknowledgements to the Institute of Administrative Management.

professional golfer from Kent who had not been quite good enough to become a successful tournament professional. Realising this at the age of twenty-one, he attended the University of Loughborough and took a diploma course in Sport and Recreation Management. He gained the job at Beaumanor after responding to an advertisement in a golfing magazine.

Bernard was a good golfer, and personable and confident. He had few anxieties about taking this job, as he felt that his lack of management experience would be compensated for by the wealth of experience on the established, elderly club committee.

The committee consisted of five members: Carew Bell, a partner in the local solicitors' firm and a founding member of Beaumanor, who was the chairman; Norman Hewish, who was a senior sales manager with a local paint factory and was club secretary after nine years' membership; Maude Bell, wife of Carew and captain of the ladies' team; Jerome Blair, men's captain and local police inspector; and the club groundsman, George Nugent.

The existing committee had interviewed three candidates before choosing Bernard on a majority, rather than an unanimous decision. On appointing him, they had given him a job description with the following areas of responsibility:

1   To provide professional golf tuition to the club and to run the professional's shop on the course, with a part-time assistant at weekends.

2   To advise the club committee on all matters relating to the management of the club, including

  (a) Development and membership.
  (b) Relations with town and community.
  (c) Catering.
  (d) Finance.
  (e) Administration.

When Bernard is appointed, it is agreed that he will work within the existing practices for three months before submitting a report to the committee for discussion.

When Bernard joined, membership was at 500, having dropped from 800 three years earlier. It was clear that the reasons for this decline had to be diagnosed and remedied, or the club would be unable to survive.

During his introductory three months, Bernard is shocked by some of the problems of the club. While the course is in a good state of repair, the clubhouse is badly decorated, with a leaking roof in the men's changing room. Bernard notices that less than one-third of members shower and change at the club, the majority preferring to drive home. This has severe effects on bar takings. He also notices that the club tradition is for ladies to play only from Monday to Thursday; none are seen on the course on weekends, although ladies represent 28 per cent of the club membership.

A further problem of the club is that, despite its fine course and beautiful natural setting, there are no regional or invitation tournaments held there. The only competitions are internal club ones, or friendly matches against neighbouring clubs.

No local schools are involved with the club and there is no junior section.

The club has never advertised in the local press, preferring to gain membership by word of mouth recommendation through organisations such as the Chamber of Commerce and the Rotary Club.

Bernard also notices that, just as there are relatively few women players at the club during weekends, it is extremely rare to see children at the club, despite the fact that there are a number of suitable play spaces, and scope for development.

Bernard found that administration in the club was lax, which surprised him in view of the high proportion of businessmen in the club. He found that there were frequent clerical mix-ups, including double bookings of tee-off times, the absence of a regulated system for collecting subscriptions and fees, and separate accounting practices – none of which were very professional – for the club catering (bar and restaurant), the professional shop and the club as a whole. This he traced to the fact that the catering was traditionally supervised by the one lady member of the club committee, while the professional shop was the responsibility of the professional (now himself) and other income was controlled by the club secretary. An outside accountant, a business associate of Norman Hewish, was paid a fee annually to present the club accounts.

The head chef, Alphonse, who had been employed by Maude Bell, could not adequately account for the cash he used to buy vegetables at the local wholesale market. Maude spoke affectionately of Alphonse, and told Bernard that restaurant management was an art to be left to Alphonse.

The seventeen-year-old trainee groundsman, having telephoned in one morning to report sick, was seen that afternoon causing a disturbance at a televised football match. Bernard threatened him with dismissal if he ever again reported sick when he wasn't, whereupon the trainee's father, a friend of Carew Bell, promptly complained about Bernard's 'victimisation' of his son.

It was then announced that construction of the final section of the city's ring road would begin in the spring. This would form a crescent around the outer edge of the suburb, the club and some 200 acres of farmland owned by the city council and let to two tenant farmers. The city council had proposed selling off the land for some £10 million, granting planning permission for developers to build some 1600 houses. It was estimated that this would increase the suburb population by 5000 to 30 000. Bordering some of the ring road would be a small industrial estate of warehousing and distribution units. The unit bordering the club grounds would be used as an indoor cricket centre. A local cricket star, Frank Milburn, who had played for England, was behind this. He had proposed (a) re-routing part of the golf course to allow construction of a joint enlarged car park and (b) reciprocal membership arrangements.

The local city council had proposed that Beaumanor be extended as a joint venture with themselves to become a leisure centre with an indoor Olympic-sized swimming pool plus a play pool. The hard tennis courts would be covered for extensive year-round use and the club bar, restaurant and other facilities in the manor house be opened to non-members, whilst members would get discounts, some booking priorities and retain some private club rooms.

Some of the managing committee were interested in the enlargement proposals but Bell and Blair, two of the founder members, had had enough. They were demanding an extraordinary general meeting to persuade members to turn down these proposals. 'We want a golf club to entertain business associates and to relax with friends', said Bell. 'I don't want children running all over the place and I certainly don't want club premises being used by lots of non-members.' 'I agree,' said Blair, 'that's not what we set out to do. Things have gone too far already.'

One committee member, Norman Hewish, was appalled with the administrative situation and with the attitude of some members. 'The annual subscription is now £120. We are no longer a small club that can get by with seat of the pants style management. We must use spreadsheets on a micro and do proper budgeting. If we go into joint ventures we'll need to know what's happening.' He has come to you and asked you to produce a formal report, 'designed to persuade the committee to improve the way we do things in this club'.

Analysis

1 Identify and list the problems that the golf club had in the following areas, prior to the arrival of Bernard:

    (a) Internal communication between officials and staff.

    (b) Communication between officials and membership.

(c) Communication between the club as a whole and the community.

2   Is there a causal relationship between any of these?

3   Identify any psychological or institutional factors that are likely to make Bernard's task of communicating with the existing committee members a difficult or delicate one.

4   What factors in the structure and organisation of the club appear to impede good communication between members?

Planning and solving

- What is to be accomplished?
- What needs to be eliminated?
- What needs to be improved?
- What needs to be corrected?

Exercises

1   Bearing in mind the need for tact, write a letter of warning to Paul Davies, the trainee who was absent at the football match.

2   Design a circular to be sent by Bernard to all local secondary schools, informing them of the facilities of the club, and offering midweek golf and group lessons.

3   Prepare a briefing paper (see Glossary) to be circulated to the membership, from Bernard, outlining the main benefits and drawbacks of possible co-operation with the indoor cricket school. The briefing paper is designed as a preliminary to an extraordinary general meeting (see Glossary) of the club to discuss the project.

4   Bernard would like to expand the club by developing the following areas:

(a) Women's golf.
(b) Outside, commercially sponsored tournaments.
(c) Children's facilities.
(d) A junior section.

He realises he cannot move on any of these points until he has a sense of the members' feelings. Design a questionnaire (see Glossary) that will enable him to measure opinion across the club on the above issues accurately and inoffensively.

5   Compose a covering letter to be sent to each member accompanying the questionnaire in which the need for change is tactfully but forcefully made.

6   Produce a poster for circulation in all local libraries advertising the facilities of the club.

7   Outline an organisational structure befitting the club that would enable effective decision-making by the committee and by the full-time officers – Bernard, Alphonse and Nugent. Be sure that decision-makers are accountable to

subscribing members. Express this structure by means of an organisation chart.
8   Prepare an information report for the committee on how a microcomputer
could benefit the club. Explain what applications are possible in the club and
how possession of of a micro would change, simplify and improve the affairs
of the club. Advise the most suitable way to acquire a system, within budgetary
constraints of £3000.

11 · Beaumanor Golf Club (2)

This chapter is designed to exercise the following skills:

1 Understanding of the main features of a formal meeting.
2 Ability to function as chairman, secretary, or ordinary member of a formal meeting.
3 Ability to produce a suitable agenda, to provide the foundation for a successful meeting.
4 Ability to write minutes.
5 Ability to make effective oral presentation of facts.
6 Ability to detect and express weaknesses in the arguments of others.
7 Ability to engage in constructive discussion, leading to majority conclusions.

Note

Prior to working closely on this chapter, it may be useful to examine the notes on the following topics in the Glossary at the back of the book: meetings, committees, chairman, secretary, minutes.

Introduction

During Bernard's first two months at the club, he notices that many members appear preoccupied by the possible joint ventures with Frank Milburn's cricket school, and with the local council. He detects that members appear to have no real confidence in the ability of the club's existing committee to resolve the situation promptly, and more than one member informs Bernard that 'no real discussion will take place; Carew will just decide and push it through next summer's AGM'.

Bernard feels that he would like to have a full discussion with the committee on a range of matters. While the most important items of concern are the two possible joint ventures, he is also keen to discuss the club-house facilities, the problems of membership and the club's accounting.

He therefore asks for a meeting of the club committee to be held, to which the other officers agree. However, when he telephones Norman

Hewish, the club secretary, about organising the meeting, Norman tells him, 'Don't worry about an agenda or anything. We're a small committee and it will be more suitable and effective if we chat on a free-wheeling basis. Everyone is very impressed with your work, and keen to support you. See you in the clubhouse at 7 p.m. on Sunday night, then.'

Hewish explains to Bernard that the club traditionally holds informal meetings between 7.00 and 7.45 p.m. on Sunday evenings, prior to the Sunday club supper at 7.45 p.m. While Bernard feels that the allotted time is brief, he feels compelled to agree and accepts the scheduling. He duly arrives in the committee room of the club-house for the meeting at 6.50 p.m. on the Sunday in question. The other committee members arrive soon afterwards, and the meeting begins on time at 7 p.m. with the following participants:

Carew Bell – Chairman
Norman Hewish – Secretary
Jerome Blair – Men's Captain
Maude Bell – Ladies' Captain and Catering Secretary
George Nurgent – Groundsman
Bernard Jones – Club Professional

CB: Good, well, glad to see everyone here promptly. I think before we do anything else, we ought to offer Bernard an official welcome. This is the first committee he has attended since joining the club full-time, and on behalf of everyone at Beaumanor, Bernard, you're very welcome and we're delighted with the job that you're doing for us. Now, I think this meeting is very much at your initiative, so perhaps you'll tell us what it is that you want to discuss.

BJ: Thank you, Mr Bell. Actually, there are a number of subjects. I know we are due to have a meeting after my first three months, but I thought it was a good idea to get together before then. The things that concern me are the possibilities of working jointly, both with the council and with the Milburn Cricket School, then the clubhouse facilities, the membership and the issues surrounding all of the club's accounting.

JB: Quite a few issues. We always look at accounts at the AGM, of course. That's only another two months. Are there urgent problems, or could it wait until then?

NH: I think we should try to discuss everything on Bernard's mind. It is really his meeting, and I'm sure we'll have time for everything on a semi-formal basis. No need for too much procedure tonight.

CB: Agreed, we'll try to cover it. Now, Bernard, let's lead off. What first?

BJ: Perhaps I could start with accounts, as we're on the topic already.

I am a bit worried that we seem a bit disorganised; that is to say, we really seem to be doing three lots of accounts instead of one. I'm doing the books for the pro shop. Well, that's simple enough; but this really ought to be tied in, I think, with the accounting for membership subscriptions, which Norman handles, and the bar and catering, which I believe Mrs Bell supervises.

MB: It has always worked pretty well in the past, Bernard. I mean, the club still exists and makes a small profit. What do you see as being the exact problem?

BJ: Well, I think too much of the bar and catering business is done on a daily cash basis, which is a bit old-fashioned. If we opened regular accounts with our suppliers, and settled on perhaps a monthly basis, we'd find it easier to record and analyse, and we'd get the benefit of negotiating discounts with regular suppliers, depending on the volumes. In fact, this is the system we use for buying golf equipment in the pro shop, and it works very well.

NH: Yes, that's a point. And if the club is going to expand and start dealing with others, we really must brush our act up and get a bit of uniformity.

MB: We haven't agreed any of these joint ventures yet. I think you're jumping the gun, and could Alphonse manage all this account business? It might rather cramp his style, you know. He likes raking round the market, and striking cash bargains.

CB: Yes, that's true. It has worked all right in the past.

JB: This can't really be discussed in isolation. We've got to look at it from the viewpoint of the future. It seems we're likely to merge with Milburn. He's got a very well-equipped bar and kitchen, with microwave ovens. He gets his supplies in direct, pre-packaged. He doesn't have to pay a chef like Alphonse, all he needs is a couple of part-time kitchen hands and the electricity to work the dish-washer. I'm sure we can use his kitchen facilities, and then bring our accounting into line with his. But at the moment, until we've decided the nature of our co-operation with him, I really don't think we should amend our existing methods. We might have to do it all again in a few months.

MB: Jerome, you must surely see that our members won't want this pre-packaged food. One of the attractions of our club is the freshness of the food, its closeness to home cooking. Our members won't like pizzas wrapped in cellophane and that sort of thing.

CB: That's true. We must at all times remember our membership and the atmosphere of our club here.

NH: I think we are getting off the point a bit. Bernard wanted us to discuss the problem, as he sees it, of our accounting not being properly integrated. I, for one, think he's got a point.

BJ: The problem with the catering is, quite frankly, that I am finding it very hard to keep proper track, as so much is done on a cash basis. Where last night's bar takings are buying today's vegetables, and there's no real record of the size of bills, well, there are a lot of problems there a modern club shouldn't tolerate. I mean, a lot of potential for abuse, for a start.

CB: Bernard, I really think we are a modern club. If you look at our members, they're not all elderly like me, you know. And golf clubs are not dance halls; you have to angle the practices of the club to the users. And does it really matter if the accounts are done in cash? I mean, surely the important thing is that the food is good.

JB: Yes, and the food is good. I think we've probably agreed that we can't make any sensible changes until we find out the situation with Milburn. I move we shelve this discussion on accounts until the AGM, or perhaps until Bernard submits his report.

NH: You're missing the point. Bernard is suggesting something about the whole way in which the club is organised and run, about the need to modernise it and integrate its separate functions. We should be discussing this in more detail.

CB: Well, sorry, Norman. Time is getting on and I can't help but agree with Jerome. But let me say this; it certainly shows that Bernard has a keen eye for organisation, and we're all grateful to him for raising it. We'll look at it again, perhaps at the AGM. Now Bernard, what next?

BJ: Well, the buildings really are a worry. The level of facilities here does not compare well with other clubs in the region, and we really do need to spend, I would think, about £40 000 modernising the changing rooms, improving shower facilities and replacing the roof. I'm sure the club could borrow the money long term to spread the load. But it really does need immediate discussion. We're not, I don't think, going to rebuild membership without this modernisation.

JB: I'm sure you're right, Bernard. We can't carry on with these very poor facilities. If we don't move on it, we will lose more members, thus have even less money, and be in a spiral of decline.

NH: Quite true, and we could usefully cost improvements to the pavilion. But equally, there are the proposals of the council to be considered. If we look hard at the leisure centre scheme – which we haven't yet done in committee – and I don't know why – this gives us another option, with the chance of top class facilities. And remember that with a local authority partner, we'd have a ready-made source of finance.

MB: Yes, but does the club really want to borrow up to its eyeballs? With today's interest charges, it could be ruinous. I know the clubhouse isn't marvellous, but surely the course is the crucial factor in the golf club. That's why people join; if they want luxury showers, they go to a sauna.

CB: And the course is certainly one of the most interesting and well maintained for miles around.

BJ: Oh, I agree. I have no anxieties about the course itself. But I feel we must offer our members more and attract new members.

JB: But the local authority leisure centre will be a complete disaster. The nature of the club would change overnight, and the membership would desert in droves. If you have all and sundry coming in, with nothing but a local council to control it, the place will go down the drain.

NH: There's a bit of contradiction there, Jerome. The membership can't be collapsing if all these people are coming in, can it?

JB: You know perfectly well what I mean. We'll have juke boxes, chewing gum, people playing in jeans, drugs, I shouldn't wonder . . .

MB: Well, we just will not have that sort of change here. The club cannot do it. The members won't have it.

NH: You are both over-reacting. Remember that, even if we do allow public access through the local authority, it will be controlled, and the club members would have exclusive use of the course at weekends.

BJ: Yes, that's true. There are many part public and part private courses, and it's always possible to safeguard the club members in some way.

CB: No, no, dreadful. I can see us all queueing up to tee-off on Sundays, and deserting the course to the local yobs the rest of the week.

NH: You exaggerate! And remember, even to the public, we'll be charging at least £7 for a round of golf. We won't get time wasters at that price.

JB: Norman, you're talking about it as if it's already happened. For my money, it isn't going to happen. I'm quite sure the members won't have it. You wait for the AGM and you'll see.

NH: Look, it's a law of survival; you adapt or you die. The area is changing around us, with the new road, factories, a population growth. If we don't sense these trends and move with them, and make the most of our opportunities, then we won't survive more than five years.

And it's a terrific opportunity for the right sort of growth. Golf should be attracting more types of people and more young people. The council scheme needs to be put fully and properly to the members and I'll be doing it at the AGM.

CB: Well, I'm sure the AGM will be very interesting. The more we talk, the more I feel we do need to wait for the AGM, and to consult the entire membership there. This has been a very useful chat and Bernard has raised some important issues. On all your behalf, I'd like to thank him for what he is doing. We'll certainly look forward to reading his report in a month or so, and discussing it then. Thank you all for attending.

Analysis

1 To what extent was this a formal meeting?
2 In what way might a written agenda have helped the proceedings? Justify your answer by reference to the transcript of the meeting.
3 To what extent did the nature and progress of the meeting reveal the underlying organisational problems of the club?
4 What weaknesses do you see in the arguments of *either* Jerome Blair *or* Maude Bell?

Planning and solving

1 Imagine that you are in the position of Bernard Jones. You would like the next meeting to be more productive than this one. Apply the following considerations to the committee meetings (with the transcript as an example) rather than to the problems of the club as a whole:

- What needs to be improved?
- What needs to be eliminated?
- What needs to be introduced?

2 How far are the inefficiencies of the committee linked to the traditions and operations of the club as a whole?

Exercises

1 Write a critique of the performance of Carew Bell as committee chairman in which you explain how his shortcomings affected the outcome of the meeting.
2 Identify at least two points where useful discussion broke down in the meeting. Explain clearly how it broke down and how such a breakdown might have been averted by either the chairman or the secretary (see Glossary.)
3 Produce a written agenda (see Glossary) for the meetings.
4 In groups of six, conduct a role play of the meeting, using the agenda produced in (3) above. Operate the role play on the basis that majority conclusions must be reached, and that the meeting must be role-played within half an hour. Take notes of the meeting as you participate.

5   On the basis of your notes, and of the section on 'Minutes' in the Glossary, produce the minutes of the meeting.

6   Select any one of the issues confronting the meetings. Prepare an oral summary of the key points to be considered, and explain your own views on the subject. Deliver this presentation to the other members of your group.

12 · The London Borough of Southden Housing Department*

This chapter is designed to exercise the following skills:

1 Appreciation of the significance of physical layout of an office to working relationships and to the quality of communication.
2 Appreciation of the difficulties of internal communication between employees of differing levels of seniority.
3 Appreciation of the importance of the flow of information and of documents within an organisation.
4 An appreciation of the importance of administrative support systems.
5 Writing an open letter.
6 Writing a recommendation report.

Introduction

Southden is one of the largest of the boroughs of inner London, with a population of 230 000. While there are some suburban and affluent areas at the southern boundaries of the borough, much of the borough suffers from the typical inner city problems of unemployment, poor housing and general decay.

Southden Council employs a total of 6000 people within the borough, and has an annual turnover of £125 million. The council is the biggest employer in the borough. With local elections due in eight months, the council leader, Margaret Hawkins, is particularly keen to project an image of professionalism, efficiency and caring to the local community. She is aware that the council's image could be improved, particularly in the local press. She, therefore, holds a meeting with the council's public relations officer, Warren Roe, as a result of which she sends the following memo to the director of each of the council's major departments: Planning, Housing and Estates, Social Services and Parks and Open Spaces.

The memo comes as something of a surprise to Michael Lockyer, Director of Housing. He has been aware that his department has a

* Acknowledgements are due to the Institute of Administrative Management, the London Borough of Lewisham and the *Lewisham and Catford Mercury* for material used in this case study.

MEMO

To: Planning, Housing and Estates,
           Social Services, Parks and
           Open Spaces

From: Council Leader   Date: 27 March 198X

Re: Public Relations Policy in Pre-Election Period

You will be aware that the borough elections take place within six months.
It is vital that we are re-elected, as many of our programmes would
be terminated or changed if the opposition takes power, with disastrous
results for the borough.

Therefore, we need to project the very best public image possible until
the election. Following a meeting with Southden's PR officer, will
you please implement the following policy immediately:

1 Any complaint received by a department must be brought to the attention
   of a Principal Officer within 24 hours of receipt.

2 All complaints must be brought to the personal attention of the
   departmental director - or his assistant director - within 48 hours
   of receipt.

3 All complaints to be answered personally by the Director or Assistant
   Director of the appropriate department - within 72 hours of receipt.

4 No complaints to be discussed with the press or general public by
   any council employee below assistant director level. All press
   communications must be routed through Warren Roe.

5 Departmental directors are entirely responsible for informing their
   staff - at all levels - of this policy.

Margaret Hawkins

Margaret Hawkins

---

particular need for public relations, as complaints to the press about
long housing waiting lists, unfair distribution of housing, and poor
decoration and repairs, are frequent. However, he has not previously
worked closely with Warren Roe (their offices, while both technically
within the Town Hall are in different buildings, and Roe does not sit
on the Housing Committee, chaired by Lockyer). Additionally, he
has never thought of involving the Public Relations office in handling
housing complaints. These have been the responsibility of Gail
Ferrera, one of his Principal Officers.

The organisation of the Housing Department

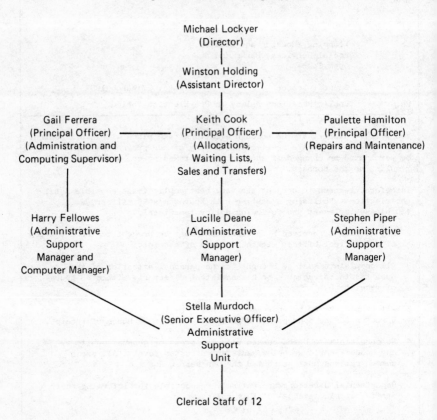

The administrative Support Unit, headed by Stella Murdoch, consists of eight clerks, two of whom specialise in accounts and book-keeping, and four secretarial assistants, who are typists, and who additionally conduct any general administrative support required by the directorate, or by one of the Principal Housing Officers, who will express his administrative needs through his Administrative Support Manager. One of these clerks, Jean McDougall, handles general correspondence for the department.

The department, therefore, has a clearly ranked management structure that works from a common pool of administrative support in the interests of saving costs.

The Housing Department, therefore, has a total staff of twenty-one and occupies an entire floor at Southden Town Hall. The bulk of the offices are open plan, housing all the administrative staff. However,

The Southden Housing Department

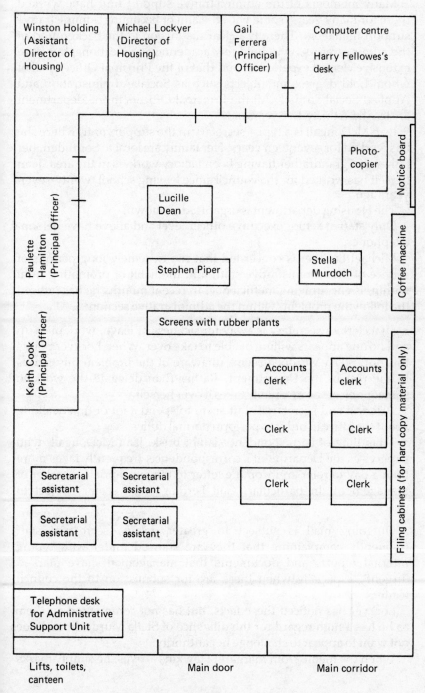

the Principal Officers each have a private office adjoining the open plan area, as does Michael Lockyer and Winston Holding.

Many members of the administrative support unit have worked there for many years, some with the aim of becoming administrative support managers. There is a clear distinction in the background of the administrators, who hold few academic qualifications, but have extensive clerical experience, and that of the Principal Officers, all of whom hold degrees in subjects such as Social Administration and Applied Social Studies. All the Principal Officers in the department are less than thirty-five years old.

Jean McDougall is a typist/secretary in the support unit, where she has worked for seventeen years. Her family are local to Southden, her father and grandfather having been factory workers in the area. Jean herself has worked for the council since leaving school twenty-seven years ago.

The Housing department is organised as shown.

Only staff at senior executive officer level and above have personal telephones.

Michael Lockyer is concerned that the extremely long periods of service of his administrative staff, and the habit of promoting from within, is encouraging inefficiency. In recent months he has noticed the following problems within the administrative section:

1   If a clerk or secretary is away for sickness or leave, work piles up and no one appears willing or able to take over. When Lockyer points this out, Stella Murdoch seems unaware of the problem this causes to the rest of the Department. Rather than delegate the work to someone else, she invariably takes it over herself.
2   Clerical and secretarial staff seem to spend a lot of time walking about the office in order to perform normal duties.
3   Handling of correspondence is not brisk. Jean McDougall, who supervises the Department's correspondence, frequently takes more than a day to refer an incoming letter to the appropriate member of management. In particular, Gail Ferrera's mail seems subject to delay.

Outgoing mail is subject to greater delays, secretarial staff frequently complaining that they are snowed under with typing internal reports and documents that management have marked 'urgent', especially when these are for submission to the council leader.

Lockyer has noticed these facts, but has not commented on them, as he has a high regard for the diligence of Stella Murdoch, and does not want to appear to challenge her authority.

When the memo from Margaret Hawkins arrives, he simply marks it 'Attention All Staff' and pins it on to the office notice board.

On 4 April 1986, a letter dated Wednesday, 2 April arrives addressed simply to 'The Housing Department' and is placed on Jean McDougall's desk for attention. She is away sick on Friday the 4th and Monday the 7th, and opens the letter on Tuesday the 8th. The letter is a complaint from Tom Brown, tenants' leader of the Bellham Estate, complaining about the council's failure to clean up graffiti from the estate. The letter threatens 'an organised demonstration' if there is no action within a week.

On reading the letter, Jean realises that it should be forwarded to Gail Ferrera for attention. But, due to her personal dislike and resentment of Gail, she keeps the letter all day, depositing it on Gail's desk only at 5.30 p.m., following Gail's departure for a meeting.

Gail herself does not look at the letter until Wednesday, 8 April. She then urgently confers with Pauline Hamilton, who telephones the council painters, and books an appointment for the following day for the estate to be cleaned up. However, when Pauline then telephones Tom Brown, it is too late. A demonstration has begun, well supported by tenants, and timed to coincide with the day that the local newspaper goes to press.

On Thursday, 10 April the local newspaper features the following story.

Sit-in gets action

Angry tenants and their children who staged an all day sit-in at Gate Housing Office last week to protest about their housing conditions claim a party of workmen later arrived on their estate to carry out a clean-up operation.

But the tenants from the Bellham Estate fear it could be a council ruse to prevent their being accepted as top priority for rehousing.

It was in February 1981 that the tenants who claimed they were living in intolerable conditions first demanded action.

On Tuesday, Tom Brown, leader of the Bellham Action Group said: 'Today teams of painters have appeared on the estate to paint out the graffiti that's been there for years and I hear the council's housing chairman is due to visit the estate tomorrow.

'We want to be classed as top priority for rehousing.'
(*Southden Mercury*, 3 April 1986, p.1)

Lockyer is telephoned at 11 a.m. by Margaret Hawkins, who is furious. He immediately requests an explanation from Jean McDougall, correspondence clerk, who defends herself with the following statement:

"Well, you see, Mr Lockyer, we get very cut off from the managers in the Housing Department. I mean, they're young people, they haven't got the roots in the area that we have. They don't want to listen to us or talk to us, they've got their high-flown university theories, and they don't seem to very interested in what we've got to say. You can say I don't get on with Miss Ferrera, but it cuts both ways, and I've been here a lot longer. And in the borough a lot longer, too. Now I didn't see the memo from Mrs Hawkins that you put on the board. I never do look at the board, anyway. The notices stay up there for years, and I must say I never look at it. We do feel a bit cut off really, as if the administrative staff are second-class citizens. Now, as for all these problems with the newspaper, I'm sorry if it's my fault in any way, but it's never really one person's fault. Anyway, Mr Lockyer, you know how long I've been working here and how much I like the Housing Department. I will try to speed up the allocation of letters in future.'

Analysis

1 How adequate and appropriate was Margaret Hawkins' memo?
2 Fully consider Lockyer's onward communication of the memo to his staff. Comment on his communication skill here, and factors that may have influenced his decision.
3 What does the incident show about the problems of notice boards as a medium of internal communication?
4 What psychological and personal factors impede successful internal communication within the Housing Department?
5 To what extent were Lockyer's problems of his own making and to what extent were they caused by the structure and practices of the council as a whole?

Planning and solving

- What needs to be accomplished?
- What needs to be eliminated?
- What needs to be improved?
- What needs to be introduced?

Exercises

1 Analyse the existing document flow within the Housing Department and identify weaknesses. Begin a document flow for incoming letters that will simplify and speed the turnover of documents.
2 Draft an open letter from Michael Lockyer to the editor of the local newspaper, in response to the article on the Bellham Estate.

3   Study the layout of the offices. Make a list of the elements in current layout that are positively harmful or potentially harmful to successful internal communication.

4   Redesign the office layout. Explain your reasoning for any changes you have made.

5   Write an explanation of the weaknesses in inter-departmental communication within the council exposed by this case. Explain how such weaknesses might be eliminated.

6   Produce some proposals for amendments to working practices within the Housing Department that would minimise the division between administrative and 'professional' staff and increase the quality and efficiency of communication.

   Submit these suggestions in the form of a recommendation report to Michael Lockyer.

13 · Asmart Ltd – the Spring Offensive*

This case study is designed to develop and exercise skills in the following areas:

1 Appreciation of the communication problems and human problems involved in the use of new technology in a workplace.
2 An understanding of house style and corporate image.
3 Appreciation of staff relations in a retailing context.
4 Market research and interpretation of statistics.
5 Appreciation of the relevance of cultural background in working relationships.

Introduction

Asmart is a three-year-old hypermarket on a fringe of town site at Basildon, Essex. It is one of fifteen hypermarkets in the UK owned by the American group Associated Marketing, who are keen to expand and improve their presence in the UK. They have sent four of their best executive managers from their Philadelphia headquarters to spend eighteen months as Store Manager of their four 'flagship' hypermarkets. The Basildon store is one of these, and is taken over by 34-year-old Marty Rosen, who has a degree in Marketing from an American university, and eleven years US management experience. Marty has not previously worked in or visited the UK, and he displaces the existing Store Manager, 44-year-old Geoff Willetts, who will work as his deputy.

Rosen inherits a store with some difficulties. A snowy winter and high local unemployment have depressed turnover, and drastic markdowns have been needed to dispose of large stocks of children's clothing and tinned food. Rosen is convinced that poor marketing is to blame.

Another growing problem is shoplifting and pilferage, which have risen to 4 per cent of turnover, and one of Rosen's first actions is to dismiss an assistant for stealing forty cigarettes, a move that causes

* The assistance of the following organisations in the preparation of this case study is gratefully acknowledged: the Institute of Administrative Management, the *Grocer*, the Economist Intelligence Unit.

A smart hypermarket management structure

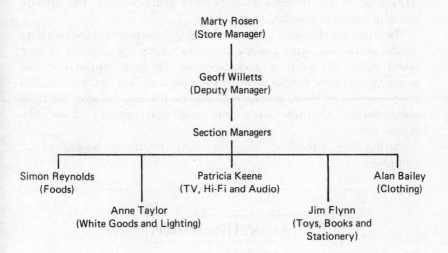

Each Section Manager has a supervisor and a number of
assistants ranging from seventeen in the Foods division to two in White Goods
and Lighting.

some resentment, especially as Willetts was in the habit of issuing a
written warning to all first offenders.

Rosen also feels that Asmart suffers from a weak and anonymous
image in the town, and decides on a major public relations drive
during the spring months of March, April and May. The campaign is
to involve newspaper advertising (budgeted at £4000 for the three-
month period), the design of a new logo, free carrier bags, and
distinctive uniforms featuring black top hats and bright red bow ties
for all front of store staff. Rosen is also determined to introduce a
clothing section for the 18–30 and 30–55 age groups.

He realises that he does not have floor space for both, and consults
Willetts about the final decision.

Willetts has reservations about many of Rosen's proposals, but is
resolved to work consistently under him.

Rosen is particularly concerned at the long checkout queues that
develop. He feels that these are costing the store a significant amount
of business, and that queues could be shortened drastically by
introducing new technology and by improving the performance of
checkout attendants. He decides to take personal responsibility for his
planned changes, and to assign Willetts to a purely administrative,

backroom role for the crucial three months, which he terms 'The Spring Offensive'. Reluctantly, Willetts agrees. Rosen is confident that the key to success in his project is direct communication with the workforce, some tougher management attitudes and the speedy introduction of new technology.

The trial period begins 1 March. Rosen spends much of the morning on the store floor with a stopwatch, examining the amount of time taken at the checkout by each operator. He later reprimands two assistants in public for not wearing their top hats, and finally conducts spot searches on three employees who are leaving the store for their lunch break. All three are found to be carrying only their own possessions.

During the afternoon, the following memo is issued to all employees:

Asmart Hypermarket

MEMO

To: All Staff

From: Marty Rosen, Manager   Date: March 1st 198X

We are starting a three-month drive to make Asmart the TOP STORE IN THIS TOWN. There is much to be done. Would you please note the following points, which are operative from 9 a.m. tomorrow.

1   All employees will be obliged to submit to security searches by
     specialist security staff at any time. A room will be made available,
     and there will be security staff of both sexes.

2   Anybody not wearing full company dress at any time is liable to
     immediate dismissal. We must improve our image!

3   Our checkout queues are far too long. From April 1st we will be
     introducing the No-loss Electra Tape system on all our stock. This
     will speed checkout and cut theft. The Deputy Manager, Mr Willetts,
     will be circulating details to you.

4   Any member of non-security personnel who apprehends a shoplifter
     will be eligible for a £100 cash bonus on the conviction of the
     offender. As from tomorrow, we will prosecute ALL shoplifters.

5   All section managers must brief supervisors on this memo, and discuss.
     Section Managers will meet in my office at 9 a.m. on March 4th
     for discussions.

Let's go everybody; this is the SPRING OFFENSIVE to make ASMART THE BEST.

Alan Bailey, Section Manager for Clothing, calls a meeting of his four assistants and supervisor to discuss the new measures. The response is generally negative, assistants feeling that the uniform, while perhaps appropriate for delicatessen staff, is not fitting for their section. Additionally, one of the assistants, Tim Francis, is particularly annoyed at the increased security, and informs Bailey that he will agree to be searched only when leaving the premises, and that he proposes to visit his local Citizens' Advice Bureau to check on his rights. Bailey informs Rosen of the discussion, and is told to 'be firmer'. Bailey therefore decides to draft some constructive proposals from his own section as an alternative to Rosen's memo.

Simon Reynolds encounters great resistance when he introduces the memo to his section. Nine of his assistants do checkout shifts; all are alarmed by the prospects of re-training, and feel threatened by Rosen's new approach. Reynolds personally supports the move to Electra Tape, and suggests to Rosen that he, Reynolds, should compose a pamphlet outlining the advantages of the new system, and of the new technology in general. The pamphlet will be circulated to the whole staff. Rosen agrees, but stipulates that the pamphlet must outline the case *for* new technology, must anticipate and counter likely objections, and must give authentic examples of work situations where new technology has been implemented and has improved employment and career prospects. Reynolds is told to 'make it persuasive and readable'.

Patricia Keene is particularly sensitive to the problem of security, as losses are especially costly to her section. However, she is strongly against the aggressive policy of Rosen, and decides to brief her team, and present alternative proposals to Rosen.

Jim Flynn, the Manager of the Toys and Books section, constantly had to deter juvenile shoplifters, and has always pursued a policy of handling the problem internally. He is horrified by the proposal for a £100 bonus, and foresees a public relations disaster for the store if a member of staff is rewarded by Rosen for prosecuting a young person, particularly if the local press becomes involved.

Analysis

1   Outline the weaknesses of Rosen's memo.
2   Discuss how far Rosen's management style was studied to the organisational structure of Asmart, Basildon.
3   In what way were Rosen's American attitudes an asset? In what way were they a liability?
4   What particular internal problems could be foreseen for 'The Spring Offensive'? To what extent did Rosen foresee them?

Planning and Solving

1   Put yourself in the position of Geoff Willetts. Identify and list all the separate problems caused by Rosen's arrival at the store.
2   List any difficulties likely to lead to a severe worsening of working relationships within Asmart.

No loss technology: something special in store for shoplifters

For twenty years we've built up a special relationship with shoplifters by putting them out of business. In big stores such as in the major stores of London, Milan, New York, Paris and Tokyo we're not very popular with thieves.

After all, we introduced electronic security tagging in the 1960s, and our technology leads the way. Take our low cost No-Loss Electra Tape, for instance. This multi-purpose strip, suitable for hard and soft articles, is virtually invisible in use, and can be built in to goods during manufacture. It is the first ever EPoS compatible tagging system, designed to provide instant bar code scanning and security strip deactivation at the point of sale – simultaneously. This unique development permits accelerated checkout without compromising security.

So it's easy to see we have something in store for shoplifters. In fact, we've been helping retailers to deter them for as long as anyone else.

Call us to discover how we can speed up your point of sale business, deter shoplifters and help electronic stock control – all simultaneously.

No-Loss (UK) Ltd,
Barleyford, Marlow Way,
Wycombe, Bucks AY7 4GH.
Tel. 96843 5864

Exercises

1   Read the advertisement for No-Loss Electra Tape. As Willetts, write an explanatory paper for all staff to read (maximum 175 words).
2   As Alan Bailey, hold a discussion group with your section (four assistants) to try to draft some constructive alternative proposals to those of Rosen's memo. Write your proposals up in memo form, addressed to Rosen.
3   As Willetts, study the population forecast for the UK from the Economist Intelligence Unit. Use the information as the basis of a memo to Rosen, advising on whether Asmart should specialise in clothes for the 18–30 or the 30–55 age group.
4   As Simon Reynolds, research and write a brief paper on the opportunities of the new technology for the staff of Asmart.

Table 7   Forecast of UK Population by Age Group,[a] 1983–98

% of population

Age Group	1983	1989	1993	1989
Total population				
0–14 years	19.8	18.6	19.7	20.4
15–24 years	16.4	15.3	13.2	12.0
25–44 years	26.6	28.7	29.1	29.2
45–64 years	22.3	21.5	22.4	23.1
65+ years	14.9	15.6	15.6	15.3
Total *'ooo persons*	56 377	56 640	57 028	57 533
Males				
0–14 years	20.9	19.9	20.8	21.4
15–24 years	17.2	16.1	13.9	12.6
25–44 years	27.5	29.6	30.0	30.2
45–64 years	22.4	21.7	22.6	23.3
65+ years	12.0	12.7	12.7	12.6
Total *'ooo persons*	27 430	27 597	27 825	28 121
Females				
0–14 years	18.8	17.9	18.7	19.3
15–24 years	15.6	14.5	12.6	11.4
25–44 years	25.8	27.9	28.2	28.3
45–64 years	22.1	21.3	22.2	23.0
65+ years	17.7	18.4	18.3	17.9
Total *'ooo persons*	28 946	29 042	29 203	29 411

a. The forecasts are based on 1983. The 1985 forecast was 220 000 lower than the actual 1985 population, which suggests that future years are also underestimates. However distribution by age groups is not significantly altered.
Source: Government Actuary's Department; retail business estimates for Northern Ireland projected population in the forecasts.

5   As Willetts, research the cost of full-page and half-page advertisements in a weekly local newspaper. (Use your own local newspaper as a guide to rates.) Design both a half-page and a full-page advertisement for the store, and present proposals for spending £4000 on newspaper advertising throughout the spring offensive. Present your findings in the form of a recommendation report to Marty Rosen.

6   As Patricia Keene, write a recommendation report on security, in which you

suggest some discreet but effective ways of handling the problem.

7   As Jim Flynn, write a memo to Rosen outlining your concern about the proposed bonus system for anyone apprehending a shoplifter. Consider the likely effects of the scheme on customers and staff, especailly if the press were to become involved.

8   Design a logo for Asmart, to be used in all advertising, carrier bags, and on any own-brand products.

Appendix 1: Glossary

The following terms, used in the text, are briefly explained below:

Agenda

An agenda is a list of items for discussion and decision by the members of a formal meeting. An agenda is usually composed by the members of a committee, who submit their topics, in writing, to the secretary prior to a meeting. The secretary then circulates the agenda to the committee members, who are then able to prepare for discussion.

Briefing paper

A briefing paper is a concise explanation of the facts or background to a particular issue that is used to inform those responsible for decisions. There are no standard conventions for the layout of such papers, but many are written in the form of an extensive memo.

Chairman

The formal title awarded to the most senior member of a committee, who is often elected from within the committee, or by a parent body. He has the responsibility of controlling all aspects of discussion, in particular attending to the following points:

- to ensure that all members of the committee have the opportunity to contribute to debate and decision-making.
- to ensure that no one member, or no small group of members, is able to monopolise debate at a meeting.
- to ensure that the committee covers all the points prescribed in the agenda or programme for the meeting. Failing this, a chairman should arrange an extension of the meeting, at a time and place agreeable to the committee at large.
- to ensure that neither too much nor too little time is spent on any one topic.
- to ensure that the individual expertise of committee members is called upon when necessary.

- to define clearly the limits of topics under discussion.
- to ensure that all committee members understand the facts of an issue before voting.
- to avoid unnecessary friction and tension between committee members in the event of disagreement. This means that a chairman will often be the agent of compromise in the case of serious disagreement between committee members, in certain cases to give a casting vote if opinion is divided equally.

Check question

A type of interview question asked simply to *confirm the expectations and assumptions* of the questioner. It requires only a brief answer. For example, 'And I believe you learned stock control techniques in your previous post with us?'

Circular

An explanatory leaflet, designed to be read by a large number of people. As such, circulars need particularly to be clear, unambiguous and concise.

Closed question

A type of interview question. See Appendixes 2 and 3.

Committee

A group of more than two people, appointed by a parent body, which meets at a pre-arranged time and place to discuss matters within given terms of reference. A committee generally has a chairman and a secretary.

Dialogue

A sustained conversation between two people, in which the roles of speaker and listener interchange.

Document flow

The system for movement and transfer of different types of document from one person to another within an organisation. Flow may begin with the arrival of external documents (such as letters) into the organisation, or with the creation of new documents by particular individuals or groups within the organisation. The flow may end up with the despatch of documents to targets outside the organisation, or in a file, or as waste paper.

It is important to note that there may be several different routes of flow for various copies of a single document that needs the attention of more than one officer.

Double crown posters

These are large and striking posters used for advertising purposes, usually within retail stores.

Extraordinary general meeting

A meeting of all the directors and shareholders of a company called in order to discuss an issue of exceptional importance and urgency that requires resolution before the annual general meeting.

Information reports

Reports that follow the standard sequence of reports (terms of reference, procedure, findings, conclusion) but which do not make specific recommendations for action to the reader(s).

Interview questions (types)

See Appendixes 2 and 3.

Job description

A list of the skills and duties involved in a particular job. Drawn up by management, it is used at the selection interview stage, and later for staff appraisal.

Meeting

A gathering of two or more people met at an agreed time and place to discuss and possibly decide questions of common interest.

Minutes

An official record of the proceedings, motions and resolutions of a committee. The Companies Act obliges every company to record and keep minutes of meetings of its directors and managers.

Minutes are usually the responsibility of the secretary or clerk of the meeting. They are often set out in the following way:

1 Date, time, place of meeting.
2 List of those in attendance.
3 Minutes of last meeting.
4 Matters arising from minutes of last meeting.
5 ⎫
6 ⎬ Items of business with details of decision.
7 ⎭
8 Any other business.
9 Date, time and place of next meeting.

Open questions

A type of interview question. See Appendixes 2 and 3.

Ordinary member

A committee member who does not have the responsibilities of the chairman or secretary, but who is entitled to speak, vote and raise motions for dicussion by the committee.

Organisation chart (organogram)

A chart demonstrating the organisational pattern of a company or concern. Usually in the form of a 'tree', it will indicate the way in which different sections relate to one another, and the pattern of seniority from top to junior management. It is also likely to reveal the key decision-making networks of an organisation. (See Chapter 5, p.33, for an example.)

Personnel specification

A profile of the 'ideal person' for a particular job, in terms of their qualifications, skills, experience and temperament, used by management in selection interviewing.

Press release

An official written statement on behalf of an organisation that is circulated to the press for information and publication.

Point of sale advertising

Advertising that accompanies a display of goods for sale within a shop, such as sweets, car accessories or washing powder.

Probe question

A type of interview question. See Appendixes 2 and 3.

Questionnaire

A series of standard questions aimed at a specific target audience to elicit the views, beliefs or behaviour of the target audience. Questions must be simple and avoid the possibility of vague or inadequate answers.

Recommendation report

A report similar in structure to an information report, but with an additional, concluding section in which recommendations are made.

Reflective question

A type of interview question. See Appendixes 2 and 3.

Role play

An exercise by which a workplace situation is acted out and further developed by participants for purposes of study. The objectives are either to develop confidence, ability and experience in the participants, or to attempt to further explore and predict certain elements of the situation being studied. Role play is a teaching and learning technique used extremely widely, especially in training for employment that involves dealing with the public.

Secretary

The member of a committee with the responsibility for circulating the agenda prior to the meeting, recording the discussion and decisions, and writing the minutes following the meeting.

Stock control

The monitoring of levels of stock within production or marketing types of organisation. Stock control is useful for predicting likely levels of orders required, managing cash flow and minimising wastage on storage space and transport costs.

Appendix 2: Types of interview question

Questioning

Asking the right questions is half the battle in getting the required answers. Think before phrasing a question and ask yourself which is the most effective way of asking it. The following types of questions will be useful:

Type of question	Example	Usage
OPEN	'Why did you decide to join the snooker club?'	There are questions that cannot be answered 'yes' or 'no'. They encourage the interviewee to expand and do more talking. It often elicits feelings and attitudes as well as facts. To be sure of asking an open question – remember to always prefix it with why? when? what? where? or how?
CLOSED	'I understand from what you've been saying that you like snooker. Is that right?'	A question to be answered 'yes' or 'no. This question summarises, and can bring the conversation back on to course if it has wandered. It enables the interviewer to tie up one part and move on to the next. It also helps to check mutual understanding quickly. Can be used to try to quieten the garrulous interviewee – but often does not succeed!

Type of question	Example	Usage
SPECIFIC	'On what day did you join the snooker club?'	Ask for specific information. There is only one correct answer to a specific question. Try using a lot of specific questions on a talkative interviewee or a 'waffler'. This is the only way of being sure of getting the facts you need – be direct.
REFLECTIVE	'I find it difficult to know in what order to pot the colours.' 'Pot the colours?'	Reflects a statement or question by rephrasing it and sending it back to the other person. This technique keeps the interviewee talking and often giving more information in depth on a subject they have just finished talking about. It also avoids personal involvement or bias on the part of the interviewer if a direct question is asked of them it is not wise to answer.
PROBE	'I think it's disgraceful that the snooker club has closed down, don't you?'	Here the required answer is indicated in the question. It is bad if used inadvertently. All the interviewer receives is reinforcement of his/her own ideas and learns nothing of the interviewee's. However, it can be well used as a test question to check a person's knowledge and attitudes. It can also be used as an easy question in the initial stages of the inter-

Type of question	Example	Usage
		view for a very nervous or young person – to settle them in.
HYPOTHETICAL	'If the snooker club were to close, what would you do?'	Good for use in selection interviewing – to test out reactions and speed of thinking – dealing with problems.

(Taken from Janis Grummitt, 'Interviewing Skills', Industrial Society, 1980)

Appendix 3: Preparing for an interview (candidate)

General preparation

First analyse the company or companies that might possibly employ you, and the jobs you might possibly obtain. Having decided on the position or positions you would like to obtain and the companies to which you would like to apply, prepare a personal data sheet and a list of your qualifications. Find out, if possible, with whom you will have the interview and what form the interview is likely to take.

Analysing the company

A company analysis will enable you to eliminate jobs where you think you would not fit in or be happy. It should also help during your interview, if you are asked the almost inevitable question, 'Why do you want to work for *us*?'

Try to include in your analysis as much as you can of the following data about the company:

Present Status. How old is it? How large? Is it financially stable, expanding or declining? What are its business policies? What distinguishes it from other companies in its field?

Organisation. How is it organised? Where are its plant, office(s), subdivisions? Who are its executives?

Products and Services. What products and/or services does it offer? What is the prestige of these products or services? What competition do these products have? How are these products or services regarded by users?

Personnel. How many people does it employ? Does it offer any kind of training scheme? What are its policies on salaries, promotion, benefits?

Most of the above information can be obtained from booklets, brochures and annual reports issued by the company. Additional information can be obtained from trade journals and business magazines, *Who's Who*, business directories, registers, guides and catalogues available in your library. (The *Bankers' Almanac and Yearbook* and the *Times Issuing House Yearbook* are particularly useful.)

You may be able to get valuable help from friends – especially if they work for the company or know someone who does. An inspection of the plant may also be possible.

Analysing the job

The employer may think you better fitted for a position other than the one you apply for. Also, if there are no openings in your special field, he may ask you to take another job temporarily.

Prepare a job analysis which answers the following questions:

(a) What education and/or special training is required?

(b) What experience is necessary or helpful?

(c) What personality traits are essential? Does one work mostly with things, with people, or about equally with both?

(d) What are the duties of the position? What skills, abilities and aptitudes does it call for? What disadvantages does it have? Does it promise a career? Is it a dead-end?

Personal data

Prepare a personal data sheet, a summary of factual material about yourself, and have it handy for reference. Keep it up to date. Some modification of this could be sent along with your letter of application. The sheet will also be useful to refer to when filling in application forms. Re-read it before an interview and refresh your memory of names and dates. The following items are suggested by questions most commonly asked on application forms:

- Name, address, telephone number.
- Age, date of birth, place of birth, nationality.
- Marital status: name of wife or husband; number; relationship and age of dependants.
- Immediate next of kin: full Christian names and surname, address and relationship to you.
- Education and training: name and type of school(s) from the age of eleven, giving dates. Main subjects studied; diplomas or certificates gained. University or technical college (full time), giving dates. Main subjects studied; degrees, diplomas or certificates gained. Part-time education, giving dates. Main subjects studied; degrees, diplomas or certificates gained.
- Membership of technical or professional associations.
- Territorial or reserve commitments.
- Details of present and previous employment, including service in HM Forces. Addresses of previous employers, dates of employment, positions held, description of duties, salaries, reasons for leaving.

- Special skills: business, technical, artistic, knowledge of foreign languages.
- Details of any serious illness or disability.
- If you are a disabled person, give your registration number and the expiry date of your certificate.
- References: names, addresses and telephone numbers of at least two people, not relatives, who know you socially or in business; their occupations and the number of years they have known you.
- Hobbies and interests.

Also, work out an inventory of your assets (and liabilities). Answer honestly the questions below. This will help you to decide between jobs as well as preparing you for the interview:

- What sort of work do I find most interesting? What kind of work do I dislike? e.g. contacting people, working with my hands, working on ideas, writing, experimental work, outdoor work, talking to groups of people, giving orders, following instructions.
- What special skills or aptitudes have I?
- What is the most outstanding accomplishment of my business career? Of my social life? What other business or social accomplishments am I proud of?
- What activities have I taken part in, socially or at school, that will help me in business?
- What is my aim in life?

(Taken from W.R. Gondon and E.W. Mammen, *The Art of Speaking Made Simple*, Heinemann, London.)

Further case studies and reading

Case studies

Further case studies may be obtained from the following sources:

The British Association for Commercial and Industrial Education
16 Park Crescent
London W1

The Institute for Administrative Management
40 Chatsworth Parade
Petts Wood
Orpington
Kent BR5 1RW

The Institute of Marketing
Moor Hall
Cookham
Maidenhead
Berkshire SL6

The Royal Society of Arts
Murray Road
Orpington
Kent BR5 3RB

Reading

The following texts are useful extensions of many of the issues raised in this book:

Michael Argyle, *The Psychology of Interpersonal Behaviour*, Pelican Books, Harmondsworth.
Douglas Ehninger, Alan H Monroe and Bruce E Gronbeck, *Principles and Types of Speech Communication*, Scott, Foresman & Co, Illinois
Charles B Handy, *Understanding Organisations*, Penguin Books, Harmondsworth
Thomas A Harris, *I'm OK, You're OK*, Pan Books, London
Sheila May, *Case Studies in Business*, Pitman Publishing, London
Margaret Wolff and Graham Collins, *Communicating at Work*, Thomas Nelson, London